# DALLAS TOUGH

## HISTORIC TALES OF GRIT, AUDACITY AND DEFIANCE

Josh Foreman and Ryan Starrett

THE
History
PRESS

Published by The History Press
Charleston, SC
www.historypress.com

*Front cover*: A cowboy keeps watch over a herd of cattle as the Dallas skyline rises in the distance, 1945. *Library of Congress*.

*Back cover*: Dorothea Lange photographs a poor family who has broken down outside Dallas en route to Arkansas. They have "[n]o food and three gallons of gas in the tank." 1936. *New York Public Library*.

First published 2021

Manufactured in the United States

ISBN 9781467146081

Library of Congress Control Number: 2020945745

*Notice*: The information in this book is true and complete to the best of our knowledge. It is offered without guarantee on the part of the authors or The History Press. The authors and The History Press disclaim all liability in connection with the use of this book.

*This book is dedicated to:*

*The fellows of Gregory Hall, especially Jimmy Early, Carlos de la Garza, John Leonard and Mike Watson. And to the professors at the University of Dallas who had the patience to put up with and educate the fellows of Gregory Hall. And to the teachers who inspired the professors, most notably Homer, Socrates, Plato, Aristotle, Augustine, Aquinas, Dante, Houseman and Dostoevsky. Thank you for the camaraderie, the lessons and the True, the Good and the Beautiful.*

*And to Herbert and Sharon Foreman, who provided for their grandchildren a country haven in Raymond, Mississippi, and who nourished those grandchildren with vegetables from the garden, stories, patience, company and love.*

# CONTENTS

# Contents

# PREFACE

This is a collection of twenty-three little-known (or forgotten) stories from the history of Dallas. They are by no means exhaustive or definitive. In fact, many of these chapters are open to alternate interpretations, and every chapter can be expanded and improved. It is our hope that these brief stories spark a more general interest in Dallas's rich history and lead to more scholarly development.

# ACKNOWLEDGEMENTS

We would like to thank all those historians, researchers, archivists, teachers, artists and photographers who came before us and paved the way for a project like this. We thank them for allowing us to stand on their shoulders to see the history of Dallas through their own work. We would like to extend a special thanks to those directly involved in our project—Joe Gartrell and Ben Gibson, acquisitions editors at The History Press; Richard Starrett for the editing and advice; the librarians at Mississippi State University's Mitchell Memorial Library for sourcing and acquiring books about Dallas from other libraries; the redditors at r/guns for providing insight on the weapons used in Texas's early days; Internet Archive and its partners for scanning, storing and sharing many old and valuable books; the users of Wikimedia Commons for making freely available their photos and artwork; Yale University's Beinecke Library for sharing its collection of documents and images; the Library of Congress, National Archives, and Smithsonian Museums for sharing their collections of documents and images; the Metropolitan Museum of Art and Rijksmuseum for leading the way in digitizing and sharing great works of art from the past; the New York Public Library for making many items from its collection freely available online; Ancestry.com and its partners for scanning, storing and sharing vast collections of birth certificates, death certificates, city directories, census records and many other documents; and newspapers.com for creating a revolutionary and indispensable research tool.

## Acknowledgements

We would also like to thank our constant supporters: Dena Kinsey and St. Joseph Catholic School in Madison, Mississippi; Dr. Terry Likes and the Communication Department at Mississippi State University; the MaxxSouth Digital Media Center at Mitchell Memorial Library for making its recording studios freely available; the local booksellers who promote and host us whenever we release a book: John Evans and his staff at Lemuria Books in Jackson, Mississippi, and Scott Naugle and his staff at Pass Christian Books in Pass Christian, Mississippi; Holly Lange and the organizers of the Mississippi Book Festival for always including us in their excellent festival; Barbara Webb for always showing up for our signings; Dierdre Payne and St. Richard Catholic Church in Jackson, Mississippi, for hosting and encouraging us; and our families, who are our steadfast readers, encouragers and patrons (Ryan and I are great writers—our mothers told us so). Thank you.

## Part I
# BLOOD AT THREE FORKS

## THE HUNGRY GEORGIAN

Staring into the tangle of oak, hickory and pine across the river, young Richard Sparks saw his fortune and his doom. That side of the river—the west side—was the genuine frontier. Creek Indians lived there. Tattooed and black-clad guerrillas, their septums pierced with rings, came from that side, looking for horses to steal and people to kill.[1] Sparks's grandfather had been unlucky. He had gone out hunting turkeys one day and a Creek had shot him down—the same year young Richard was born. His grandma had kept the man's bloody shirt, pierced by a musket ball, until the day she died.[2] Danger came from the west side of the river. Sparks's doom was there.[3]

Sparks lived on the east side of the river, in a fort his family had built. He lived on the white side. It had been Creek land, too, up until a few years before. Now it was called "Georgia." The Creeks on the west side of the river hunted to fill their bellies. The whites hunted too, and they raised great herds of cattle. A mark of their superior culture, they thought.[4]

There was so much grazing land on the west side of the river. So much game. The whites took their cattle to the west side, and while they were there, they blazed away with their guns. They "destroyed the game so bad, that they can hardly find a turkey to hunt," one witness lamented. The whites brought their dogs, too, and wiped the forests clean of bears. That was the fortune part of Sparks's vision. That Indian land held riches in furs, meat, land and forage—if the white man had the gall to take those riches.[5]

*Above*: The Oconee River near present-day Athens, Georgia. *Library of Congress*.

*Right*: *The Creek Indian*, by Frederic Remington, 1906. *Library of Congress*.

Sparks grew up in his home on the Oconee River hearing stories about how his grandfather had been killed by the Creeks and about how his father had done his share of fighting against the Cherokees during the American Revolution. And he heard stories of distant places—the Mississippi Territory—that held different Indian tribes called Choctaw, Chickasaw and Biloxi. New lands, new opportunities.[6]

Sparks was just coming into adulthood when his family decided to sell their land in Georgia and make for the Mississippi Territory. His arrival in Mississippi coincided with a growing national desire to see Indian tribes in the Southeast evicted altogether. The state and territorial boundaries of Georgia, Tennessee, Alabama and Mississippi were growing to encompass tribal lands. Indians were given a choice: accept individual allotments of tens or hundreds of acres each and gradually become U.S. citizens or leave the Southeast and settle west of the Mississippi.[7]

The Creeks, who had been fighting against white intrusion for decades, signed an allotment treaty. So did the Chiskasaws and the Choctaws. As the land east of the Mississippi was brought into the national fold, whites took advantage, buying Indian allotments or simply squatting on them. The allotment treaties effectively deprived eastern Indians of their autonomy, and many began the journey west.[8]

Sparks arrived in Marion County, Mississippi, in 1811. He and his family had left the foothills of the Appalachians and the Creek Indians behind. His new home was in the plains of south Mississippi. The land was flatter, but the trees were the same, mostly. Oak, hickory, pine—the same trees he had grown up with in Georgia.

He married, fathered several children and served as a trustee in his Baptist church. He was a farmer, cattleman and slave owner. He stayed in Mississippi for two decades, buying and selling land and taking on roles of responsibility in his community. He stayed in Mississippi long enough to see it become a state. He even served as a state representative. He had made it, had found many riches. But his riches were not enough to keep him in Mississippi. His gaze again turned westward. The Southeast tribes had been forced west across the Mississippi River. Sparks would cross the river too.[9]

In about 1833, Sparks moved his family to Nacogdoches, a thriving but shabby frontier town in Mexican Texas. Nacogdoches was a magnet for rabble-rousers—it was far from the seat of Mexican power and close to the United States, and whites there began agitating for Texas independence. It was also a magnet for fortune-seekers. Vast Texas seemed to hold even more riches and opportunity than the Southeast. And none of the colonial powers had ever really wrested all that land from the hands of Indians.

Sparks, arriving in Texas, set about collecting spoils. Within a few years, he had acquired forty thousand acres through Mexican grants. The Mexican government—before it realized that inviting whites into Texas was not a great idea—had established a generous land distribution program in the 1820s to attract settlement.[10]

Sparks became a commissioner for the town of Nacogdoches. But again, he felt restless. He took over a trading post up the Neches River, far into land claimed by the Cherokees. The post was situated near salt flats, a natural spot for trading with Indians. When Texas declared its independence from Mexico, Sparks was asked to treat with the tribe. His job was to dissuade the Indians—who led a confederation with other tribes—from joining the Mexican side of the conflict. As part of the job, in 1837 he furnished a cache of goods to the Cherokees that included blankets, tin cups, knives and kettles.[11]

He also became interested in surveying around then—a skill that could enlarge his already impressive holdings. Texas's General Land Office had opened in 1838, and land speculators, anxious to snatch up the best unclaimed land in Texas, hired surveyors to venture into Indian territory.[12] Surveyors often received a cut of whatever land they surveyed. A party had set off a few days before to map some unknown land up the Trinity River. Sparks decided to join the expedition. The land he eyed was known simply as the Three Forks, because three streams converged there to form Rio Trinidad, or the Trinity River.

Sparks departed with eight or ten other men. As Sparks and his party traveled northwest, they watched as the forest—the forest Sparks had always known—became sparser and sparser. Instead of forest, trees grew along the banks of streams. And the trees were different. Where there were no streams, the land opened up into vast expanses. The expanses were filled with animals. "Thousands of buffalo and wild horses were everywhere to be met with," a contemporary of Sparks wrote about the area. "Deer and turkeys always in view and an occasional Bear would sometimes cross our path—wolves and buzzards became our acquaintances and in the river we found abundance of fish."

When they reached the Three Forks, they stared westward at something none of the men had likely ever seen: rolling hills covered by an ocean of grass. They had reached the blackland prairie. Little bluestem rose from the land in fine, blue-green clumps. And because it was spring,

*War Whoop*, from *Historical and Statistical Information Respecting the History, Condition and Prospects of the Indian Tribes of the United States*, vol. 6, 1851. *Internet Archive.*

wildflowers peeked up from the grass here and there. The men must have noticed that the soil of the flatland was dark and rich. The soil was the product of a cycle of blood-spilling and burning that went back eons. It was a farmer's dream.[13]

Sparks and his companions chose a spot in the ocean of grass off the westernmost branch of the Trinity and set up camp. One man went to fetch water. Four others went off to hunt, fish or survey. The remaining three—including Sparks—lay down and slept.

It was then that Sparks's doom finally materialized on the prairie, in the form of seventy Kickapoo warriors painted red, their hair shaved into mohawks, eagle feathers standing straight up on their heads as the men bounced on their horses.[14] The surveying compass was an object despised by the Kickapoos, and the warriors had ridden into the white men's camp to spill blood. They set eyes on Richard Sparks, held their guns steady as they rode and fired. Sparks may have been sleeping when an Indian ball tore through his skull, or he may have awoken in time to see the nightmare horde stampeding into camp, but Richard Sparks added his blood to the Three Forks that spring morning in 1838. As Sparks's life drained away into the black soil of the prairie, the other men in his camp were awoken by the sounds of horses, whooping and gunfire; they managed to scramble away from camp with their lives—but nothing else.

The members of the expedition who had been at the river or afield heard the cracks of the gunfire and knew better than to come riding back to camp. From different directions, they straggled back to the settlements, where the men who'd witnessed the Kickapoo attack told of Sparks's death.[15] Readers in Nacogdoches and Houston learned a few days later when an account appeared in papers. The papers were incredulous—the Indians on those plains were supposed to be friendly.[16]

Sparks had come to the Three Forks looking for the spoils that had always been there, in Indian land. But he and his companions were not the only fortune-seekers to have descended on northeastern Texas in the early decades of the nineteenth century. The Kickapoos—a tribe native to the Great Lakes, not the Texas prairie—had also arrived. And they were unlike other Indians Sparks had encountered in his life. They enjoyed a particularly "unfavorable" reputation among their peers. Texans thought they were harmless, but that would soon change. The Kickapoos would soon earn new nicknames—"Lords of the Middle Border" and "Texas's Greatest Enemy."

Richard Sparks had chased the frontier to the Three Forks, where in a few years the city of Dallas would grow. For the seed of Dallas to germinate, though, it would need watering with blood. Sparks contributed his, but the blood of others—both Indian and white—would be required.

# KICKAPOO HORSE LORDS

Just six months before Richard Sparks met his end at the Three Forks, the government of the newly independent nation of Texas received a report on the Indian tribes within its borders from its Standing Committee on Indian Affairs. I.W. Burton, serving as chairman, wrote the report and addressed it to President Sam Houston.

Burton's report identified twenty-six different tribes living in Texas. He named the Caddo Indians the "greatest rogues and most treacherous Indians on our frontier." The prairie Indians—the Keechis, Tawakonis, Wacos and Pawnees—were also considered treacherous. The Cherokees had signed a treaty with the Texans but could not be trusted.

When Burton turned his attention to the northern tribes living in Texas—which included the Kickapoos—he described a group of five hundred well-armed hunters and marksmen who "roam the Prairies in perfect confidence." But the report described them as rather benign; they had been in Texas for eight years, were friendly to whites and had no ambitions of settling permanently on Texas soil. In a few months, Burton's observations of the Kickapoos would prove to be grossly inaccurate.[17]

The true character of the Kickapoos would have been revealed to Burton if he had studied the past two centuries of French, British and American interactions with the tribe. In the early 1600s, the Kickapoos had shown the French—the first Europeans to come into contact with them—that they were not like other Indians. The Kickapoos were still living in the Great Lakes region then and were one tribe among several who spoke an Algonquian language and shared cultural characteristics. When the French began to establish themselves there in the 1600s, most of the Algonquian-speaking tribes—intrigued by European knives, hatchets, guns, blankets and trinkets—readily entered into trading relationships with them. The Indians settled near French forts and spent much of their time ranging for the furs the French so desired. The French introduced liquor into their cultures. The Indians' traditional lifestyles were degraded.[18] "The Kickapoos," wrote Arrell Gibson, a historian of the tribe, "were a notable exception."

The Kickapoos were downright hostile to the French, refusing to accept their presence in the region and resisting the kind of trade relationship other tribes had agreed to. Instead, the Kickapoos became "outlaws," "a rugged team of bandits who plundered French supply trains, shot down messengers and isolated coureurs de bois, massacred Indians friendly to the French, paralyzed communications in the Northwest, and, in general, threatened the dream of French empire in America." The French had found the thorn that would continually dig into their sides.[19]

As time moved on and French power in the Algonquin region waned, the British and then Americans moved in. The new colonizers, too, began to feel the ferocity of Kickapoo resistance. American independence saw a new wave of settlers moving west, and the Kickapoos found themselves again pitted against foreign, white interlopers. They resisted as fiercely as they had the French. In the first seven years of American independence, Kickapoos and other Algonquin tribesmen killed some 1,500 settlers and stole or ran off twenty thousand horses. The American governor of the area, then called the "Northwest Territory," authorized in 1790 a series of offensives against Kickapoo villages along the Wabash River in present-day Indiana. American armies razed Kickapoo villages along the Wabash. The Kickapoos rebuilt. Then the Americans returned and razed the villages again. The Kickapoos rebuilt. The Americans returned. Two years of American attacks were enough to persuade the Kickapoos to abandon their traditional homeland. They moved toward Illinois and the Missouri and Ohio Rivers—southward and westward, away from American settlements.[20]

It was there that the Kickapoos came into contact with another European power: the Spanish. The Spanish viewed the Kickapoos not so much as a threat to trade but as a potential ally against Indian tribes who were thorns in their sides (the French, too, had occasionally hired the Kickapoos as mercenaries). The Chickasaws had been terrorizing Spanish traders on the Mississippi River, and the Osages had been attacking Spanish settlers farther west. The Spanish hired the Kickapoos as mercenaries against the Chickasaws and Osages, paying the Kickapoo warriors with barrels of brandy, powder, shot and rolls of tobacco.

The Kickapoos launched a guerrilla war against the two tribes that resulted in many scalps, prisoners, horses and war trophies taken. The Kickapoo mercenaries proved to be exceptionally effective, quickly bringing the Chickasaws and Osages to treat with the Spanish for peace. But the Spanish had struck a deal with the devil. The Osages and Chickasaws had been brought into line, but the Spanish had gained a ferocious new neighbor in the Kickapoos, a neighbor whose bloodthirst could not be turned on and off with the flip of a switch.[21]

The Spaniards' new neighbors wore the skins of the animals of the eastern woodlands—deer, bear, beaver, moose and rabbit. The men were fond of shaving their hair into the mohawk style—bald on the sides with a short strip on top and a long lock in the back. To their mohawks they tied tufts of red-

Babe Shkit, a chief of the Kickapoo Indians, circa 1894–1907. *National Archives.*

dyed deer hair and the feathers of eagles, turkeys, cranes and herons. They wore loose cloth shirts and loaded their necks with strings of white beads. The women wore wraparound skirts of buckskin and knee-high leggings. They made twine from possum fur and buffalo wool. They rubbed their skin and hair with fish oil and bear fat and added red paint to their bodies.[22]

The Spaniards' striking new neighbors had waged a war against the Osages so effective that the Kickapoos had displaced them. The Kickapoos occupied the land in present-day Missouri that the Osages had called home. Again, they ran into American settlers looking west for fortune. The Kickapoos saw the American settlers as more targets for theft and murder. In a three-year span, the Kickapoos caused $33,000 in property damage. The settlers were apoplectic and demanded action from the territorial government, headed in part by the famous explorer William Clark. Clark devised a plan to reduce aid payments to the Kickapoos (which stood in 1819 at several thousand dollars per year) each time they stole horses or destroyed property. The growing presence of American settlers in Missouri was ultimately too much for the Kickapoos there to stomach, and again they set off south and west, searching for land where they could live away from white settlers.[23]

The Spanish, who had employed the Kickapoos to great effect against the Chickasaws and Osages, again devised a purpose for the tribe. Spanish officers in Texas began inviting Kickapoos to settle there, north and south of the Red River at strategic points. The Spanish, whose territorial border

Scout Mobiel, in Kiowa war-time costume *Library of Congress*.

with the United States had been moved to the Red River with the Adams-Onis Treaty in 1819, saw the Kickapoos as a potential buffer between them and the Americans; if the Kickapoos were there, maybe the Americans would not try to take more Spanish land in Texas. The Kickapoos would also serve as a buffer between the Spanish and hostile western tribes such as the Kiowas and Comanches. The Spanish promised brandy to the tribe in addition to territory and played on the tribe's hatred for land-hungry Americans. The Spanish were "gentle" governors in comparison, one Spanish official told the tribe.[24]

The plan worked, and bands of Kickapoos crossed the Red River, settling in north Texas. They had arrived just in time for another fight—again, this time, with white settlers. The battle lines had been drawn for a conflict that would, in a few years, begin taking the lives of Indians and Texans alike. The Kickapoos had arrived in Texas after two hundred years of conflict with white men—two hundred years during which the tribe saw its land crowded by whites again and again and again. For decades, they had been fleeing American encroachment. And here they were again, watching white surveyors pitch tents on their prairies. The murder of Richard Sparks was the first strike in a war that was the expression of their hatred, and it would not cease for decades.

## THE LUCKY COLONEL

Maybe, if he stood still enough, he could hear the war whoop hanging in the air from two years before—the Comanche scream, a sound that once heard could never be forgotten. Or the screams of the Parkers and the Frosts, settlers who'd come to this spot east of the Trinity River to take a piece of land for themselves. Ghosts hung around this spot like dust.

Colonel William F. Henderson looked around at the little fortress-town that had come to be called Parker's Fort—the whole thing was a series of interconnected cabins, blockhouses and walls. The fort was supposed to be Indian-proof. That's why it was built. But the Comanches and Kiowas had shown that wasn't the case. They'd descended on the fort two years before, massacring five of the fort's inhabitants, skewering a grandma and making off with white women and children. The other settlers in the fort had run for their lives. But they had returned, and now there were twelve families living there.[25]

Henderson, a cold-eyed man with a bushy beard and a mouth that curved naturally into a frown, was waiting that day for another surveyor: Richard Sparks. Sparks and Henderson would go north surveying in tandem. Henderson had been there for two days, though, and there was no sign of Sparks. Can't wait forever, he thought. He led his party of fourteen men out of the bulletproof walls of the fort.

Henderson's party made its way to Pin Oak Creek, just west of the Trinity. They were about sixty miles south of the present city of Dallas. The work of surveying required the men to fan out, sometimes breaking off into groups separated by several miles. While Henderson surveyed near the creek, he heard an unusual sound—two gunshots in rapid succession. Because guns in those days were single-shot and had to be laboriously loaded between shots, the two gunshots were suspicious. (Samuel Colt had received a patent for a revolving pistol two years before, but his pistol was not yet widely used.) A hunter in his party, a man named F. Holland, was out there somewhere, but there's no way Holland could have fired two shots that quickly. Henderson made camp, and his party passed the night with no word from Holland.

Henderson's men grew spooked. The false note in the call of a bobwhite or the nervous tic of a horse was suddenly a potential sign of an impending Indian ambush.[26] They were afraid to range out hunting and so had scarce food. Holland certainly hadn't shown up with any turkeys or deer. One of Henderson's ponies had cut its leg on an axe and bled to death. This surveying expedition did not seem to be going well. Henderson's men demanded they turn around and head back to Parker's Fort. Henderson acquiesced, but one of the men from his party, Barry, resolved to continue the work. Against Henderson's urging, Barry continued north with a few men.

As Henderson and his party made their way back toward Parker's Fort, they came across a cedar ravine, at the edge of which stood a clump of buzzards. As they approached the ravine, the men realized that their companion Holland's mangled body, stripped naked and almost unrecognizable, was the object of the buzzards' attention. The sight of the corpse sent a chill even deeper through the men. "Demoralization had set in upon their hearts like some terrible disease," Henderson would write.

With an Indian threat confirmed, the men hastened back to Parker's Fort. But Henderson, braver than his companions, could not leave Barry and the three surveyors who had accompanied him alone on the prairie to meet a similar fate. He convinced two other men to accompany him and again left the fort bound for Pin Oak Creek. They reached the creek but could not find Barry. Then they heard two dogs barking in the distance. Barry had two dogs.

*The Treaty*, by Michael Boyett. The statue stands in downtown Nacogdoches, Texas, and shows the agreement made by Texas Indians and settlers during the Texan war of independence. *Library of Congress.*

The men rode in the direction of the noise but found they were too late: Barry had been ridden down and killed by a group of fifteen Kickapoos. In a cruelly ironic twist, Barry had spotted the Kickapoos riding in the distance and, mistaking them for Richard Sparks and his companions, flagged them down with a waving hat. Barry's companions had managed to escape by fleeing through the grass toward a stand of trees and converged at Henderson's camp.

More terrified than ever, Henderson and his companions rode again, "like the Arabs of old," to Parker's Fort. They were met there by the remains of Sparks's expedition, who broke the news of Sparks's death.[27]

The Kickapoos, determined to again resist white encroachment on their land, had fired the opening salvo of a war that would last a generation. Richard Sparks had followed the frontier west as far as he could, but there were many other men in Texas like Richard Sparks—Henderson, for example. Henderson had ventured into hostile Indian territory and had lost friends and nearly his own life. But he faced a choice, just as the families of Parker's Fort had faced two years before: double down, risk injury, loss and death at the hands of hostile Indians and pursue the riches of the frontier—or cut losses, find a safer place to live within the confines of the settled lands of Texas and the United States and give up on frontier fortune-seeking. Unfortunately for the Kickapoos, Henderson and many men like him would decide that the promise of riches was too tempting and would push into their land again and again—until the inevitable settler tide rolled in and stayed.

Henderson waited a whole five months before heading back to the same spot his party had been repelled from before. This time, he took twenty-two men and a boy. They passed through Parker's Fort and made their way to the creekland north. And again, they found the Kickapoos waiting for them.

A small army of three hundred mounted Kickapoos—the bulk of the Kickapoos I.W. Burton had said were living in Texas—were there hunting buffalo. When they saw the party of white men, they weren't immediately hostile. But when they saw the men's surveying compasses—regarded as "the thing that steals the land" by the Comanches—they grew incensed and tried to persuade the surveyors that an attack on them from another tribe, the Ionies, was imminent and that they should head back south immediately. The white men disregarded the warning, and after three days of surveying, the Kickapoos attacked.

The outnumbered surveyors tried to resist, but the Kickapoo attackers all but wiped them out. "Whenever one of our men would put his head up to shoot," wrote Walter P. Lane, one of Henderson's companions, "twenty-five Indians would pull down on him." Sixteen of the party were killed, and the remaining seven—five badly wounded—spent the afternoon hiding in a ravine, their only cover some scrub bushes and a lone cottonwood tree, exchanging fire with the Indians. They escaped at nightfall, but lit by a bright moon, they were easily seen and harassed by the Indians. Henderson was one of the two men to escape without serious injury.[28]

In *My Bunkie*, painter Charles Schreyvogel depicts a group of frontier scouts being ambushed by unseen Indians. *Metropolitan Museum of Art.*

For the next several years, surveying parties spread out through Texas, moving west toward the Colorado River. "The thing that steals the land" would prove to be insatiable, and even the bloody fate of Henderson's party would not be enough to deter settlers from the Three Forks.

## THE SURVEYOR TRIUMPHS

It took a year for another luck-pushing frontiersman to return to the spot where Richard Sparks bled out on the prairie. The man was a New York Yankee named Warren Angus Ferris—a man who, like Sparks, had been drawn inexorably west in search of riches in Indian land. Ferris had traveled far west, spending six years as a fur trapper and trader in Colorado in the early 1830s. Although he had lived the life of a nomad, his true ambition was to become a wealthy landowner and settle down. "Money is the modern God worshipped by all the world," he would write to a friend. "Acquire wealth and you can accomplish anything." His ambitions drew him in 1837 to the same city Sparks had been drawn to: Nacogdoches.[29]

Ferris's land ambitions led him to regard the Indians living in the vicinity of Nacogdoches as impediments to white settlement. After arriving there, Ferris made a name for himself as a "ranger," a militiaman who responded to Indian depredations against settlers. He considered Indians to be mostly "rascally, beggarly, thieves and rogues." Soon his frontier savvy—and his willingness to fight Indians—won him the position of Nacogdoches County's official surveyor. It had been firmly established that white settlement would meet with ferocious Indian resistance, so Nacogdoches's official surveyor needed to be a fighter.

William P. King, a Mississippian land speculator in Nacogdoches looking to cash in on the Texas land grab, contacted Ferris about surveying a piece of land at the Three Forks that seemed like a promising site for a city. Ferris was to map 400,000 acres and locate a bluff overlooking the Trinity that would serve as the site of a new city called Warwick. Although Ferris was not legally supposed to accept contracts from private citizens, the deal was too appetizing to refuse. In exchange for a successful survey, Ferris would receive $900 and a one-twelfth stake in the city of Warwick. Two years after arriving in Nacogdoches, an opportunity to realize his dream of landownership had presented itself.[30]

Ferris would have been well aware that attempts to survey the Three Forks the year before had been disastrous. So, he took precautions that his predecessors had not. First, he planned to take about double the number of men compared to those who had tried on previous expeditions. Second, he wanted his party to be well armed and well provisioned. Third, he did not want his party to come into contact with Indians—period.

He set out from Nacogdoches in the fall of 1839 with fifty-five men. They advanced toward the Three Forks, but when they came across moccasin tracks, the expedition turned back. He tried again a few weeks later. Again, moccasin tracks spooked him, and the expedition turned back. A third expedition was again turned back by signs of Indians. Ferris was demonstrating a level of caution that Sparks and Henderson simply had not. His caution would ultimately make the difference between his predecessors' failure and his own success.

Repeated evidence of Indians in the Three Forks area had hurt support for the surveying effort in Nacogdoches. Ferris himself, though, was not deterred. In November, he succeeded in recruiting a smaller group of men, twenty-nine, to try once again surveying the Three Forks. Ferris and his men moved cautiously and slowly, taking twelve days to cover 150 or so miles.

Ferris's caution, however, averted a disaster that could have rivaled the surveyors' fight of the previous year. For the fourth time, Ferris's expedition found signs of an Indian presence—probably just moccasin tracks, as they had found before. It isn't clear whether the Indians were Kickapoos, but it's likely, considering that it was the same area the Kickapoos had occupied the year before. Instead of turning back, this time Ferris made the decision to track the Indians. It didn't take long for the party to find them.

The Indians were hiding in a canebrake, waiting to ambush the surveying party. A similar ambush had routed Henderson's party the year before. But Ferris's carefulness had alerted him to the trap, and his party approached the Indians with guns drawn and revenge on their minds. "We charged," Ferris wrote to a friend the next year, "and your humble servant shot one through the heart at a distance of 80 yards." The surveyors had turned the ambush, and the Indians were routed. The spoils of the battle were discovered at the Indians' camp: meat, corn and beans, axes, ropes, guns, knives and bows and arrows. Indian blood had been added to the black soil of the Three Forks.[31]

Ferris's party had won a victory, but they discovered that the Indians they'd routed were only the rear guard of a much larger group. Ferris's companions decided that staying in the area would be foolish and turned back toward Nacogdoches. But Ferris—perhaps feeling impatient, perhaps driven by longing for the land he was promised upon a successful survey—decided to stay and explore the Three Forks. Four others agreed to accompany him. The party of five stripped their supplies down to the bare minimum: food, surveying equipment, hatchets and blankets. They became nocturnal creatures, slinking around the countryside by night and sleeping in brush-covered ravines during the day. The winter months came on, and the wet and the cold made life miserable. Ferris and his four companions spent most of the winter exploring, though, before finally heading back to Nacogdoches. He had proved that the Three Forks could be penetrated—that the Indians in the area were not an insurmountable deterrent.

King, the man who had commissioned Ferris to explore the Three Forks, was happy enough with Ferris's work that he paid him in shares of his company—fifty, each worth $200. King also promised him a further $5,000 upon completion of another expedition. Ferris was back at the Three Forks that spring, doing the work necessary for Dallas to be established. And he was well on his way to becoming a wealthy landowner.

Ferris's successful penetration of the Three Forks area cleared the way for other settlers. Around the same time Ferris explored the area, another man, John Neely Bryan, devised his own plan for settling down there. He

*The Bronco Buster*, by Frederic Remington, 1895. *Metropolitan Museum of Art.*

built a crude shelter on the Trinity in 1841, becoming the first white man to permanently settle there and earning the moniker "the Father of Dallas." The Texas government built a fort at present-day Irving, intensified its efforts to clear Indians from the area and granted contracts to the Peters Company to encourage settlement.[32]

The Texas Kickapoos, who had resisted white encroachment with all their ferocity, eventually agreed to move far to the west, to the banks of the Rio Grande, where they still reside today.

Part II

# BIRTH OF A CITY

## A GOVERNOR IS SNUBBED

How quickly fortunes changed in those days.

It was a sight to behold: all six feet, two inches of Governor Edmund J. Davis riding in a buggy into Dallas's town square, escorted by a small army of Black men whom a decade before had been enslaved. And there was a white man, Jack "Shingle" Scott, walking alongside the Black men. Scott was a man who'd seen his fortunes change—one day he'd been a shingle maker who couldn't garner enough votes to gain the captainship of a Black militia. The next day he'd been the captain of that very same militia. Governor Davis's pen had made it so—ah, the efficient power of gubernatorial appointment in Reconstruction Texas.[33]

Governor Davis, a slender and poised West Point graduate who had refused to fight for the Confederacy despite being a longtime Texan (Davis had instead chosen to lead a Mexico-based Union cavalry unit), had been governor for a year. He was in town that day in August 1871 to speak to the citizens of the small town of Dallas. Or perhaps it would be fair to call Dallas *his* small town, since he had appointed the city's mayor and aldermen. Texas had officially rejoined the Union shortly after Governor Davis had taken office the year before, but democratic privileges had not been fully restored to the state's people. Governor Davis was a Radical Republican, and he had wielded every bit of power he could since taking office.

A portrait of Governor Edmund J. Davis, from *A School History of Texas* (1912). *Internet Archive.*

Much of that power stemmed from an "enabling act" passed in 1870 during the fractious Twelfth Texas Legislature. The act allowed Governor Davis to appoint more than 8,500 state positions, including the seats for Dallas's mayor and aldermen.[34] Governor Davis did not let the opportunity to hand-pick Dallas's leadership go to waste. Dallas's leaders had already been appointed by a U.S. Army general, J.J. Reynolds, by the time Governor Davis was inaugurated. Davis wanted to un-appoint some of those men and appoint others in their stead. Dallas's mayor, Ben Long, resigned shortly after Davis took power, presenting an easy opportunity to fill the Dallas mayoral vacancy with his own man. Davis chose Henry S. Ervay to do the job.[35]

Ervay had been a safe choice for Davis. Ervay was, according to a report from the time, "of the Davis party and always a Union man."[36] He was someone Davis could count on to support his Reconstructionist vision for Texas. That vision included a centralized, integrated, free public school system; restrictions on carrying firearms; the creation of a state militia that could be called on to enforce order in the case of civil unrest; granting the governor the ability to declare martial law across the state; and the formation of the state police, which would be a multiethnic police force of a few hundred that would have the power to arrest citizens when local police would or could not. Ervay was also someone Davis could count on to show the governor basic pleasantries—to welcome the governor to Dallas when he decided to drop in for a visit.

Except Ervay was not, it would turn out, a Davis man. Davis's desire to dramatically centralize power in Texas had already begun to make him deeply unpopular in the state just a year into his tenure as governor. Davis had proved that he would take drastic steps to gain legislative approval of his "pet measures," arresting and confining a group of nine opposition senators during one of the legislative sessions of 1870. Governor Davis's measures were met with much skepticism by more moderate Republicans and Democrats in the legislature, but for the most part he got what he wanted—to the horror of many across the state.[37]

Ervay was one of those turned off by Governor Davis's radical agenda. Ervay had supposedly always been a Union man, but it was also true that Ervay had worked for the Confederates during the war. For the first decades of its existence, Dallas had proved to be prime wheat-growing territory, and flour milling was its biggest industry. That led the Confederacy to select the town to be the headquarters of the quartermaster general of the Trans-Mississippi Army of the Confederacy. A previous injury spared Ervay from having to decide whether to take up arms against his adopted state, but Ervay apparently had no problem with helping to feed the Union's enemies and signed on with the quartermaster general.[38]

It was also true that Ervay had been a member of the "Immortals," a band of private soldiers that accompanied a notorious "filibuster" named William Walker on an ill-fated journey to seize control of Nicaragua. Walker, an Anglo Catholic from Nashville, hoped to reintroduce slavery to the Central American nation. His hopes evaporated when he was shot to death by a Honduran firing squad.

Ervay was rescued by the British navy but sustained serious injuries during the expedition—the same injuries that would spare him from Civil War combat. That he had accompanied Walker on such a mission suggests that he would not have appreciated Governor Davis's attempts to educate Black children, grant unconditional suffrage to Black men and even seat a Black alderman on Dallas's town council.[39]

If Davis had doubts about Ervay's feelings toward him, they would become clearer on that day in August when Davis visited Dallas with his retinue of Black escorts. The governor might have expected Ervay—ostensibly a leading Dallas Republican—to make the most basic preparations for his visit. But when Davis arrived in Dallas's town square, he found that his own party had not rolled out any sort of welcome mat. They did not prepare a stage for Governor Davis or a platform on which to speak in the town square. They did not serve drinks to the governor on the hot August day. Instead, the governor's opposition had done those things. The Democratic Party had built a stage, set out chairs and prepared lemonade.

The governor spoke for an hour and twenty minutes to a stoic crowd. He

William Walker, the "Filibuster." *Library of Congress.*

must have noticed that the town's Republicans did not offer any sort of audible support as he spoke. He certainly noticed that they hadn't prepared anything ahead of his arrival—he commented as much to some local Democrats as he left the stage. And he certainly noticed that Mayor Ervay, who was supposed to be his man, had not even had the decency to call on him in Dallas. As Davis left the town square in his buggy, a local Democrat took the stage to raucous applause, adding further insult to the governor's injury.[40]

Ervay had gone rogue, sending Davis a clear signal. Davis began plotting his revenge immediately. The all-powerful pen would be his means of retribution, he decided—he had appointed Ervay, and now he would un-appoint him and place a true Davis man in the mayor's chair.

Within a few weeks of his Dallas visit, Davis dispatched a message to Ervay: Dallas will have a new mayor soon. You are being replaced. Now kindly resign your position and hand the reins to your replacement. Or else.

But Ervay, that old adventurer's spirit stirring in his spine, was feeling rebellious. He decided that now would be the time to openly defy Governor Davis. He sent word back to Governor Davis: he would not step down. He was the rightful mayor of Dallas.

Governor Davis, not known for his gubernatorial restraint, could not abide such insolence. If Dallas's upstart mayor would not willingly step aside, the governor had the means to compel him.

Ervay had gambled that he could somehow defy the governor and come out on top. But Ervay soon found himself in a position that must have left him feeling pessimistic: sitting in a Dallas prison cell on an April day in 1872, wondering whether he'd made the right choice.[41]

## A MAYOR IS SCOLDED

It was February 1872, and John M. McCoy sat scribbling in his Dallas office. He was writing to his family back in Indiana, as he often did. McCoy had moved to the town two years before to practice law with his uncle. He might be described by the uncharitable as a Carpetbagger. The man held his pen and thought about the best way to phrase it.

"We have had some trouble in our city government," he wrote, "through the illegal removal and appointments of Aldermen by our governor. Our council was illegal for a time and of course, [that] made all their acts illegal.

Happily, for us now, we have got it all straight." Two years a resident of Dallas and already McCoy was in the middle of Dallas politics.

McCoy's terse and sanitary version of the events that had transpired over the previous weeks belied the fact that Dallas's city government was in full rebellion against the governor of the state. McCoy—a highly educated northern teetotaler who seized every opportunity to bring Dallas closer to his vision of a law-abiding, Christianized town—had nonetheless thrown in his lot with Mayor Ervay and declared himself in opposition to the state's Republican governor. "I am thoroughly disgusted," he wrote to his family.

By this point, Governor Davis had already informed Mayor Ervay that he wanted him to step aside and make way for his replacement. Davis also wanted to appoint—and did appoint—three new aldermen to the Dallas council, including a "big buck negro" who particularly irked McCoy.

At the same time, Ervay, having made up his mind to openly defy Davis, set about organizing an election to fill the same three council seats that Governor Davis had filled. The election was held, and three new democratically elected aldermen prepared to take their seats on the town council.[42]

The people of Dallas found themselves in the unique position of having two town councils—one legal and one illegal, though which was which depended on whom you asked. Dallas's leaders were showing that the town's rebellious spirit had not been crushed with the Confederacy's defeat. A few days after McCoy sent the letter to his family, a different letter arrived at Dallas Town Hall, informing Ervay that Davis's appointments must be respected. His aldermen must be reseated.

McCoy, who had thrown in his lot with Ervay, believed that the council with the Davis appointments was the illegitimate one. And his opinion was important, because within a few days of writing his letter home, McCoy would be elected Dallas's first town attorney. Of course, the town council that elected him was, according to the governor, illegal. Nevertheless, McCoy was about to take a leadership role in Dallas, and he would use his legal expertise and position to do everything he could to help his soon-to-be imprisoned mayor.

McCoy appealed to the state attorney general and a Supreme Court justice for protection. They both declared Davis's appointment illegal, leading Davis's appointees to "gracefully retire." But Davis continued to push, and McCoy began planning an appeal to the Texas Supreme Court to protect Ervay.

Governor Davis's judicial connections proved to be more effective than McCoy's. Davis refused to sit idly by while Dallas's mayor and aldermen defied him, and in the weeks following the town's "illegal" election for aldermen, Davis paid a visit to District Judge Hardin Hart, a bulwark of Republican power who lived and held court in Dallas. Hart was a man whom Davis had appointed and whom Davis could actually count on. Hart lacked a formal education and had grown up in the mountains of Virginia. He had paid dearly for his loyalty to the Union during the Civil War.

Hart and his brother had relocated to Texas by the time of the war's start. His brother joined a Union regiment that fought in Arkansas and was hanged for treason by the Confederacy. Hart himself was "severely abused and roughly handled," although he managed to survive the war while remaining in Texas. He accepted federal judgeship appointments after the war, a fact that did not help his popularity. Hart was so despised by some Texans that a gang ambushed him as he traveled in 1869, severely injuring him. The ambush cost Hart his arm.[43]

Hart was reviled by the Ervay cadre, which considered him a "villainous judge…owned body and soul by the governor." Although Judge Hart had not joined the rebellion against the Union, that rebellion had cost him much, and he had long since given up caring about the opinions of his traitorous fellow Texans. He must have had little patience for local politicians who continued to rebel against their superiors. Governor Davis asked Hart to produce a mandamus ordering Ervay to step aside. Hart did, but Ervay still refused to give up his office. Hart ordered the Dallas sheriff to find and arrest Ervay. McCoy did everything he could to prevent the arrest, even reassuring the sheriff that, from a legal standpoint, he was not obliged to follow Judge Hart's orders. The sheriff decided that he'd better obey Judge Hart. Governor Davis had shown, once again, that he had the means to get what he wanted.[44]

In the years before Ervay's arrest, when he was just an aspiring livery operator, his popularity in Dallas had been recorded in local newspapers. He hosted fetes for Dallas's young socialites—parties that lasted into the early hours of the morning. One newspaper proclaimed him "universally popular." He was popular and, apparently, also susceptible to pressure from his Dallas peers. Facing jail time, Ervay considered giving up the office of mayor. But the citizens of Dallas "generally" asked him to resist and accept imprisonment. They would cheer him every moment he was in jail, and the Texas Supreme Court, they assured him, would set him free before long. Ultimately, Ervay chose not to disappoint his peers. "He braved it like a man," McCoy wrote home to his family in another letter, "and into jail he went."[45]

Another account reveals the mood of Dallas's populace as Mayor Ervay headed to jail: "He went to jail followed by the good will of every honest man and with the prayers of all men and women who believe there is a final reward for the just."[46]

By the next morning, McCoy had already finished a petition to the state Supreme Court and was riding to Austin to deliver it. McCoy wanted a writ of habeas corpus, which would effectively get Mayor Ervay out of jail. Ervay would have to travel to the court in Austin, where the Supreme Court would decide whether he could be legally jailed for defying Davis.

As it turned out, the Supreme Court had just ruled on a very similar case. The law was settled—Governor Davis did not have the right to un-appoint mayors. The Supreme Court wrote to Judge Hart, asking him to free Ervay immediately. Hart complied, and Ervay stepped out of his cell a free man— and mayor once again, as well as thenceforth a "hero" in Dallas.[47] He had spent three days in jail.

## THE MOTHER OF DALLAS

The Dallas of the early 1870s was on the cusp of greatness, but it was yet a rough little town. Although downtown would soon be bustling, a citizen could find himself "knee-deep in wildflowers" in prairieland just outside the city. The city was a market town for cotton and wheat growers, busy with stagecoach traffic even before the arrival of any train. But people still lived uncomfortably, sharing unpainted, clapboard "residences in the sand," as one early witness put it. One young man who had just moved to Dallas in 1870 wrote about how he shared a bed with other men for warmth and rejoiced when he had simple vegetables like onions and cabbage to eat with supper.[48]

Dallas had no streets, "just places where people hoped streets would be someday," another witness described. "Many muddy bog-holes hindered walking, but there were a few board walks around the courthouse." The 123 Black men who marched into Dallas's town square alongside Governor Davis's buggy on the fateful day of his visit in August 1871 were said to have been conscripted construction workers, forced to march by the "dirty creature" Shingle Scott. Newspapers reported that the men had not even wanted to escort Governor Davis but had been threatened with fines and jail time if they'd refused.

The Black men had been working that day on a construction project that would completely change Dallas. They had been building a suspension bridge over the Trinity River.[49] Since Dallas's earliest days, the Trinity River had been an obstacle to travel. Dallas lay on the east side of the river and was cut off from the south and west by the river's forks. South and west were important directions—Houston, Austin, Galveston and San Antonio all lay to the south, and Texas was developing westward as the frontier receded.

One of the earliest and most influential settlers of Dallas had recognized early that people would pay to cross the Trinity. That settler was Sarah Horton Cockrell, who with her husband, Alexander Cockrell, purchased land and a license to operate a Trinity River ferry from John Neely Bryan. Dallas at that time was tiny—around 430 people lived there, with another 1,740 calling the county home. The downtown area of Dallas consisted of fewer than ten buildings, among them a hotel, a tavern and a log courthouse. The Cockrells badly wanted the land and the license to the ferry, paying Bryan $7,000.

If Bryan hadn't begun operating a ferry on the Trinity in 1841, it's likely Dallas never would have grown into a town. Because Bryan's ferry was there, the government of the Republic of Texas chose the spot to be a major crossroads. The government wanted to encourage white settlement in North Texas and authorized in 1841 the construction of two new roads: the Preston Road, which would run from Austin to the Red River, and the National Central Highway, which would run from the Dallas area to the northeast corner of Texas. The two roads were built, intersecting near the Bryan ferry. Dallas became a natural stop for travelers on the two roads.[50]

A photo from around the turn of the twentieth century showing the Trinity River when it is swollen and out of control. *Library of Congress.*

The Cockrells did not waste time before investing further in their river-crossing venture. They operated the ferry for two years before building a covered wooden toll bridge across the river. Although we think of bridges now as public works projects funded by governments, in those days bridges were often private ventures; proprietors could recoup the cost of building them, and then some, by charging tolls.[51]

Sarah Cockrell had accompanied her parents to Texas from Virginia and had found love in her mid-twenties when she met Alexander, a thoroughly wild man who had made his living hunting and trapping in Indian territory. Sarah and Alexander became some of the first residents of the area when they claimed a homestead at Mountain Creek, twelve miles from Dallas, in 1847. Alexander Cockrell built them a cabin out of cedar logs, while Sarah Cockrell took up the duties of a frontier wife, cooking wild game over a campfire and grinding corn with a hand-powered mill. They could not have known that Dallas—which scarcely even existed then—would become an important North Texas city in their lifetimes.[52]

The Cockrells operated their wooden toll bridge for four years and further invested in the town of Dallas, buying a gristmill, building a brick office building and beginning construction on a hotel. Then tragedy struck. In 1858, Alexander was shot and killed during an argument over money, and the wooden bridge he and his wife had built collapsed. Sarah was left without a husband and one of her chief means of earning a living. Rather than succumb to grief, Sarah Cockrell showed that adversity would not snuff out her ambition. She began operating another Trinity River ferry, this one starting and stopping at a landing south of Commerce Street downtown. It would run for another

The iron bridge of the Trinity shortly after it was constructed, 1880s. *New York Public Library.*

fourteen years, facilitating untold numbers of travelers, whose tolls made their way to Sarah's Dallas house, which served as her office.[53]

The ferry served its purpose, but Sarah Cockrell was not content. Shortly after her wooden toll bridge collapsed in 1858, she began looking for a more permanent solution. The following year, Sarah Cockrell approached the Texas state legislature with a proposal: give her a charter to build a newer, better bridge across the Trinity, and she would get it done. Plenty from Dallas were opposed to the idea of Cockrell further cementing her control over Trinity River crossings; a group of fifty-five Dallas businessmen petitioned the legislature, asking that Cockrell's charter be denied. Dallas needed a free bridge, they argued. But the legislature did not listen, granting Cockrell the new charter by a near unanimous vote.

Permission had been granted for Cockrell to begin building a new bridge, but the Civil War and its aftermath would postpone construction for more than a decade. When the time came to finally plan and build a new bridge, Sarah Cockrell aimed for permanence. To find it, she looked north to Iola, Kansas, where a company called the King Wrought-Iron Bridge Company was building bridges across the West. The company would fabricate—in Kansas—a bridge of iron for the town of Dallas. It wouldn't collapse. It might last forever. But it wouldn't be cheap, and it wouldn't be easy to transport. In 1870, Cockrell, who still owned the charter for the bridge, recruited one hundred Dallas businessmen to raise the capital for the project. They amassed $55,000 and formed the Dallas Wire Suspension Bridge Company.[54]

Although Iola was only 350 miles from Dallas as the crow flies, the pieces for the bridge would have to travel some 3,500 miles on different railroad lines and aboard different steamships before finally arriving in Dallas. They would take a month to travel from Iola to Dallas and another month to assemble once they reached Dallas. As the King company worked on the iron pieces, local workers constructed massive limestone piers for the bridge to sit on when it arrived.[55]

It was during the construction of those limestone piers, just weeks before the iron bridge would arrive from Kansas, that Governor Edmund J. Davis visited Dallas. The 123 Black men working diligently on the limestone piers—men literally building the foundation for Dallas's future growth—would receive a visit from a man with a funny nickname. They would be escorting a governor that afternoon, Shingle Scott would tell them. Construction on Sarah Cockrell's masterwork would have to be postponed for a day. The governor demanded it.

## THE TRAINS ARRIVE

Three months after Mayor Ervay was freed from jail, his town changed forever. He likely stood with a throng of five thousand of his fellow Texans on July 16, 1872—Texans on foot, horseback and piled onto buggies—a mile south of Dallas. It was the biggest crowd to have ever assembled in Dallas, and all eyes looked southward. They were straining to glimpse the first train to ever arrive, a Houston & Texas Central wood-burning locomotive pulling eight freight cars and one passenger car.

An eyewitness account from that day provided a vivid portrait: "About 9 a.m. some sharpsighted folks, gazing south, yelled 'there it comes.' First a wisp of smoke, and then the outlines of the engine shaping up, growing larger, whizzing toward us. The crowd went wild. Men whooped, women screamed, or even sobbed, and children yelped in fright and amazement."[56]

The railroad had arrived in Dallas, and just over a year later the Texas & Pacific Railroad would arrive as well, making Dallas a true crossroads—more than doubling the town's population overnight and tripling it within eight years. In 1870, three thousand people lived in Dallas. By 1880, more than ten thousand did.[57]

*Left*: The Texas and Pacific Railroad "Flier," stopping in Dallas. *Library of Congress.*

*Below*: "Locomotive," circa 1874. *Library of Congress.*

Although Mayor Ervay's short mayoral tenure is notable for his defiance of the governor, the man is responsible for something far more impactful in the long term: the luring of the railroads to Dallas.

The railroad almost did not make it to Dallas. The route of the Houston & Texas Central line had originally been planned to pass Dallas eight miles to the east. Mayor Ervay helped organize two elections to raise public funding to have the line moved to just east of the city. Dallas citizens donated $5,000 and right of way to the railroad, and the route was moved westward. Similarly, the Texas & Pacific Railroad had planned for its track to pass by Dallas far to the south. Wrangling by Dallas attorney John C. McCoy, uncle of the man who had helped Ervay through his tribulations, led to the line being moved to the outskirts of town. Dallas citizens voted to give the railroad $100,000 in city bonds, right of way and a depot where the train could stop. Ervay had been instrumental in organizing the votes and support for the railroads and passed other essential ordinances that extended the town's main street to the railroad tracks.[58]

Mayor Ervay only served for another few months after the railroad's arrival, yielding the mayor's chair to Ben Long, who had vacated it two years before to visit family in Europe. Ervay continued to serve for a decade as alderman.

Sarah Horton Cockrell, who provided the other piece to Dallas's transportation puzzle in the form of her iron bridge, continued to excel in business, amassing a fortune and earning the title as one of the true founders of Dallas.

The Supreme Court decision limiting Governor Davis's appointment powers foreshadowed the direction Texas would go as it distanced itself from the Civil War. Democrats would seize statewide power in 1872, and Governor Davis would give up hope of winning statewide election again. Judge Hart would persevere for a few more years, becoming one of the last vestiges of Republican power in Dallas. Davis would be remembered by his fellow Texans as, as one historian put it, "with the possible exception of Santa Anna, the most detested man in Texas history."[59]

## THE KILLER DENTIST

He needed fresh air. Fresh, dry air. The excessively humid climate of his native Georgia was killing him. He was destined to die young, but he preferred to put it off as long as possible. He decided to move to Dallas. Texas, he had been told, possessed dry weather and sunny skies. Only, "Dallas" wasn't exactly "Texas." Rather, it was a humid city in the eastern third of a massive state that was, in fact, dry only in the central and western portions. Unfortunately, there was little difference, climate-wise, between his new home, Dallas, and his old, Valdosta, Georgia.

Shortly after establishing his business, the business he had trained two years for at an elite Philadelphia, Pennsylvania college, he was forced to shut it down on account of his declining health.

Illustration based on a commonly used portrait of Doc Holliday from the 1880s. There is uncertainty who took the photo and whether it is actually Doc Holliday. *Josh Foreman/Wikimedia Commons.*

THE DENTIST LEANED OVER his patient. He was in the midst of one of the most basic of dental procedures: a tooth extraction. The operation would only net him fifty cents, but he had two more patients coming in later that day, one for a gold filling and another for a set of teeth. The two procedures would net him seventeen dollars in all.

The popular dentist knew how to work his customers. He had the talent and the people skills to build quite a lucrative business. He leaned over and softly whispered to his client as he worked the infected tooth free, "It is better to have good teeth than a fine set of clothes." Who knew? Maybe the man would come back later for a vulcanized rubber tooth—one of the dentist's specialties. Then, all of a sudden, the dentist convulsed in a fit of coughing. He grabbed his handkerchief and covered his mouth. Too late. Droplets of blood had already sprayed mist-like onto the face of his patient.

It was the second time that week blood had involuntarily sprayed from his mouth. It would not happen a third time. Word quickly spread, and the lunger dentist was forced to seek another vocation.[60]

TUBERCULOSIS WAS THE NUMBER one cause of death in nineteenth-century America, killing anywhere from 10 to 20 percent of the population. Often called "consumption" for the way the disease ate and consumed the body, the symptoms included a dry cough, susceptibility to pneumonia, ulcers in the throat, asthma, chest pains and an elevated heart rate. The disease was little understood during the 1870s. Some doctors prescribed whiskey; others a climate that was arid and sunny, preferably with a high altitude; and still others, persistent bathing in hot springs. A few simply recommended a life of rectitude and heroic suffering, for death was a foregone conclusion.[61]

DR. JOHN HENRY HOLLIDAY was a Georgian by birth, learned his trade in Pennsylvania, became a legend in Arizona and died in Colorado. In between, he found his avocation and vocation in Dallas, Texas.

The young dentist was never forthcoming about his reasons for leaving his connections, potentially lucrative job and relations in Georgia to head west to Texas. It might have been his diagnosis of tuberculosis, it might have been jilted love,[62] it might have been forthcoming prosecution over a shooting incident[63] or it might have been an insatiable desire for adventure.

Regardless of motive, Dr. Holliday said goodbye to family along the Georgia-Florida line and boarded a steamer in Pensacola bound for Galveston. (He took with him his uncle Tom McKey's unique knife, "Hell Bitch"—a heavy, long-bladed, double-edged knife made from a meat cleaver that his cousin had used during the Civil War.)[64]

The dentist arrived in Dallas in 1873. "He was slim of build and sallow of complexion, standing almost five feet ten inches, and weighing no more than 130 pounds. His eyes were of a pale blue and his mustache was thin and of a sandy hue."[65] Although he was a drinker, carouser and fighter before, these pastimes became more frequent once Holliday arrived in Dallas. Some doctors insisted that whiskey was a good tonic for consumption. Perhaps he began to drink under doctor's orders. Or maybe it was to forget whatever traumatic experience that made him head west in the first place. Then again, the fast life just might have been in his DNA.

If it was women he was after, Holliday had plenty to choose from. It was easy to find carnal love in Dallas. All one needed was money. Shortly after the dentist's arrival, the mayor of Dallas passed an ordinance prohibiting prostitution. Those caught selling their bodies were fined anywhere from $5 to $100.[66] (Those paying for the pleasure were arrested at a significantly lower rate. Over a one-year span in 1874 and 1875, 184 women were arrested and fined for prostitution, while only 9 men for "associating with prostitutes.")[67] The local paper became littered with notices like the following:

*"Charity Cather, prostitution, plead guilty and fined $5 and costs."*[68]

*"A colored woman, Katie Daniels, was fined $5 for being an inmate in a house of prostitution."*[69]

*"The Mayor's time and attention was chiefly occupied yesterday in fining a large number of women on the charge of being inmates of a house of prostitution. Ten fair but frail boarders at the notorious Lady Gay saloon and dance-house, were each compelled to contribute three dollars and costs toward defraying the expenses of the city."*[70]

The Colt "Peacemaker" revolver, first manufactured in 1874—the year after Doc Holliday moved to Dallas. *Metropolitan Museum of Art.*

It is certainly no stretch to assume that John Henry Holliday made at least a few visits to the houses of ill repute. After all, within a year after leaving Dallas, he began a long and contentious relationship with Kate Elder, a dancehall woman who had previously been arrested and fined for prostitution. (She had been selling herself at a house in Kansas run by James Earp's wife, Bessie. Wyatt Earp's consort, Sallie Haspel, was also arrested in the brothel sting.)[71]

The high number of transient males, the availability of making a quick dollar and the relatively low fines if caught ensured that the brothel business would continue to flourish in Dallas.

# CITY OF VICE

An 1873 *Dallas Weekly Herald* article provided a survey of Dallas the year Dr. Holliday arrived. The city was inhabited by roughly seven thousand persons, of whom one thousand were Black. There were two hundred businesses, six hotels, streetcars and a half-finished courthouse. The article concluded, "In short, the citizens of Dallas are energetic, law-abiding, educated, hospital [*sic*] charitable ladies and gentlemen."[72] The reality was a bit different.

Dallas was an up-and-coming town and, consequently, was filled with persons such towns attracted—"the good, the bad, and the ugly." The railroad had arrived in Dallas in 1872. But so had yellow fever. In fact, when John Henry Holliday first arrived, the city had just recently been freed from quarantine. Its streets were muddy. Most houses and buildings were under construction. The place reeked of muck and sawdust. And yet the city seemed promising—at least for a visionary.

Dallas had grown from 1,200 residents to 7,000 in the space of a year. It did have the railroad. It even had so many profitable cattle being driven through its streets that the town allowed pigs to roam free as a way to rid the streets of cow feces. But most of all, Dallas offered the sporting life. In particular, Main Street itself contained more than forty saloons and their accompanying opportunities for gamblers, brawlers and hourly paramours.[73]

The *Dallas Daily Herald* chronicled the city's crime over a one-year period from April 13, 1874, to April 13, 1875: "Drunk and down, 480; drunk and disorderly, 284; vagrancy, 92; theft, 34; fighting, 182; disorderly conduct, 91; carrying concealed weapons, 43; gambling, 114; resisting officers, 24; prostitution, 184; associating with prostitutes, 9."[74] Captain June Peak noted that half of the statistics were not recorded because those who could pay their fines were not listed as having been held in jail.

Other minor, but fineable, offenses were listed as well. The law in Dallas used crackdowns on gambling as a source of revenue. It was a symbiotic relationship. The *Weekly Herald* editorialized:

> *There seems to be no settled policy looking to eliminating this element* [gamblers and keno men]. *These people rent rooms, commence business and play under the very noses of the authorities, who cannot be so blind as not to know that gambling is going on contrary to the law. The thing goes on until it gets obnoxious, and then there is a sudden burst of stage indignation, and the "sports" find themselves descended upon, arrested and hurried into court, where they smilingly plead guilty, pay a nominal fine, and it is not a great while before their establishments are again in full blast.*[75]

Holliday could testify to the benevolently fickle nature of Dallas law. He was arrested in April 1874 and again one month later for gambling. He paid his fines and, like so many other gamblers, was soon back in the saloons, deck of cards or keno sheet in hand.[76]

Arguably, the most popular game for sporting men during Holliday's sojourn in Dallas was keno. A June 28, 1873 article in the *Dallas Daily Herald* proclaimed: "We haven't got a 'kourt house,' but we beat the world for keno."[77] The game was only recently introduced to Texas, but it quickly became a favorite among the city's sports. Just one and a half years later, the same paper asked, "Can anybody tell how many keno saloons, gambling hells and barrooms Dallas boasts of? Is one hundred and fifty a small estimate?"[78]

Although the keno games, and gambling in general, led to addiction, poverty and killings, the municipal authorities determined to turn the vice into a positive. They began to collect a de facto tax by periodically arresting and fining the games' participants. The fines were small enough to enable the gambler to return to his recreation until his next arrest and subsequent fine. The *Dallas Daily Herald* reported a string of arrests in a typical one-month span:

> *"Ed. Terry, another Arkansian—old enough to know better—who drops twenty-five dollars and costs for exhibiting keno."*[79]

> *"James Kirk, exhibiting keno, plead guilty, and was fined five dollars and costs."*[80]

> *"William Peters, Mike Muller and James Kirk, three good-looking young sports, plead guilty to the charge of exhibiting a little game called Keno. Each won a pot with ten dollars and costs."*[81]

Every gambler understood and accepted an arrest and fine every now and then as collateral damage. More often than not, they would be back at the keno or cards table within the week—evidently, the aforementioned James Kirk was, where he had the misfortune to be arrested and fined twice in a four-day span.

While Dallasites knew that gambling was an epidemic ("It is said by those who pretend to know that keno will re-open tonight. And the grand jury in session, too."[82]), the city tried to present the image of propriety, a truly safe, desirable place to move to, raise a family and build up a business. In short, there was a major effort to present Dallas as respectable. The *Dallas Daily Herald*, probably tongue-in-cheek, reported the arrest of several local "celebrities" for operating and playing keno:

> *The trial proceeded, witnesses were examined, and a verdict of not guilty was returned by the jury. The evidence before the court was conclusive that no keno game had ever been played in our town....We had thought quite differently, but are glad to record our mistake.*[83]

Doc Holliday was well aware of the law's schizophrenic attitude toward gambling. Aside from his own two arrests noted earlier, no doubt a number of his acquaintances also experienced the fickleness of the law. In fact, at least one of the gamblers he met in Dallas would play a significant role in the dentist's post-Dallas life. James Earp—the brother of Virgil, Morgan and Wyatt—was arrested, fined and released in December 1875:

*Captain June Peak, on his arrival home yesterday afternoon from his recent trip to Alabama, was handed an advertisement of a keno room, on the corner of Lamar and Main streets, which stated that at twelve o'clock precisely, twenty dollars extra would be given away. Captain Peak accepted the invitation and was promptly on hand at the hour mentioned with an escort of several policemen. The proprietors and employes [sic] Henry Nolan, E. Emmerson, John Clarke and James Earp, were required each to give a bond of twenty-five dollars for their appearance before his Honor the Mayor, this morning. The city authorities are very lenient with the sporting fraternity of Dallas and it behooves them to show a little modesty and instead of advertising their business in flaming handbills, to keep their daily avocation somewhat shady.*[84]

But as long as the fines remained light and jail could be avoided by promptly paying them, the sports of Dallas had little incentive to mend their ways.

DR. JOHN A. SEEGAR was a respectable man. He had a good reputation and a good business going on 56 Elm Street:[85]

DR. J.A. SEEGAR
*Can be found at all hours of the day at his old stand at Cochran's drug store, Elm Street. His office is well fitted up for the reception of ladies. I will guarantee all my work, and it shall be in the best and latest styles. I have a new automatic plugger and would like to use it. It fills teeth well.*[86]

But his partner was putting all his hard work in jeopardy. His partner was undeniably talented, as he was an excellent dentist. (The two of them had recently won five dollars at the Dallas State Fair & Exposition for "best set of teeth in gold," as well as "Best Vulcanized Rubber" and "Best Set of False Teeth."[87]) He just wasn't a good man. He'd been arrested twice in one month for gambling. And then there was the fighting. Dallasites were quickly learning about the gambler-dentist's quick temper.

Dr. Seegar simply couldn't risk his good name or that of his practice. This Dr. John Henry Holliday would have to take his dental tools with him and relocate.

DOC HOLLIDAY DID RELOCATE in an attempt to revive his practice and his name, at least for a little while. The struggling dentist moved to the corner of Main and Lamar Streets. He paid his property and poll taxes on June 1, 1874, but within weeks moved north to the more rugged town of Denison, Texas.

*Le Dentiste*, by Felix Bracquemond, 1870. *New York Public Library.*

For the next six months, he traveled back and forth between the two towns, quickly transforming into a full-time sport. The drinking and gambling and fighting continued. And so did the coughing. His acquaintances in Dallas read of his exploits in the local paper: "Dr. Holliday, and Mr. Austin, a saloon keeper relieved the monotony of the noise of fire-crackers by taking a couple of shots at each other yesterday afternoon. The cheerful note of the peaceful six shooter is heard once more among us. Both shooters were arrested."[88]

Holliday realized that there was nothing left for him in Dallas. He had tried to live as a respectable citizen but failed. His health and his attachment to the sporting life pushed him further and further away from respectability. It was time to move on.

By mid-1875, the failed dentist had moved to the central plains of Texas. But Holliday would return to Dallas in 1877 (after nearly cutting off a man's head with Hell Bitch in Denver, allegedly).[89] Shortly after returning to Dallas, he was arrested on three counts of gambling and then spent the next six months on the move. Holliday was in Breckenridge, Texas, when his acquaintances in Dallas learned of the dentist's death. The *Dallas Weekly Herald* reported, "Our reported [*sic*] was told in Fort Worth yesterday that a young man named

Doc Holliday, well known in this city, was shot and killed at Breckenridge last Wednesday by a young man named Kahn. Our informant stated that Holliday had caned Kahn and both were arrested and fined. Holliday met Kahn and attacked him again, when Kahn shot. Kahn was cleared at the examination."[90] The *Herald*'s report of Holliday's demise was premature by ten years. But it was a foreshadowing of the last decade of Doc's life.

The dentist would be arrested one more time in Dallas for gambling in September 1877.[91] He would never return. Holliday moved west and became a legend after he joined forces with the Earps and killed two cowboys at the O.K. Corral in Tombstone, Arizona. The subsequent assassination of one Earp brother and the severe wounding of another led Holliday to ride with Wyatt Earp on a vengeance tour that culminated with the death of a number of cowboys and cemented Holliday's legend as a frontier vigilante.

Holliday finally succumbed to his inevitable doom, tuberculosis, at a hotel in Glenwood Springs, Colorado, on November 8, 1887. The bleeding lungs that forced him to abandon his dentist practice in Dallas and pursue a life of cards, saloons and gunfights finally gave out. He was thirty-six years old.

Reenactors (*from left*) Aaron Gain, Zach Etter, Kyle Truhill and Bob Kenney assume the roles of Doc Holliday and other famous gunfighters in Tombstone, Arizona. *Library of Congress.*

# THE BANDIT QUEEN

She had found herself a good man. He was attractive, from a good family and was a former Confederate guerrilla, disenfranchised for his loyalty to the South. In Dallas County, the latter quality was a real mark of honor. In addition, her family (the Shirleys) and his (the Reeds) were on amiable terms. So, when eighteen-year-old Myra Shirley informed her parents that she was going to marry twenty-year-old Jim Reed, they posed no objections.

The two were married on November 1, 1866. Jim helped out on the Shirley farm in Scyene when he wasn't selling saddles and bridles in Dallas proper. He eventually planned to buy land and raise cattle and horses in Scyene.[92] But then he moved his family to Bates County, Missouri, 450 miles from Myra's own family. Less than a year later, Myra gave birth to her first child, a daughter whom she named Rosie Lee Shirley, the pearl of her mother's eye. Three years later, Belle gave birth to a second child, her son, Eddie. What should have been the happiest time of her life just wasn't. She missed home. She needed a support system.

Myra had returned to Scyene in 1868 to bury her brother, Edwin, who had been shot dead while stealing horses.[93] She was back again in 1873— this time, she hoped, for good. A lot had changed since 1866. Most notably, the Houston and Texas Central Railway had arrived, and Dallas had grown "from an obscure frontier town of twelve hundred inhabitants to a brilliant city of twelve thousand."[94] Myra needed the change. Life had not worked out among the Reeds of Missouri. Specifically, her seven-year marriage to Jim Reed made Myra seek the comfort of her Shirley family.

Jim had not been the dashing, stable man she had married back in 1866. Well, maybe dashing, but certainly not reliable, nor faithful. His dream of raising domesticated animals never came to fruition. So, he turned to crime—and infidelity.

In 1874, the year after Belle left him, Jim Reed traveled to San Antonio to pursue a potentially lucrative business opportunity: robbing the Austin–San Antonio stagecoach. He was accompanied by two partners in crime and an attractive eighteen-year-old he had seduced in Dallas named Rosa McCommas. Jim had promised to take her south and marry her. Rosa, like Myra, had fallen for Jim Reed's notorious charm.

On April 8, the three men stopped the stagecoach, six-shooters in hand. They ordered the driver and all eleven passengers to the side of the road, where they "took all their money and jewelry; broke open their trunks, gutted the mail bags, taking one of them and three of the stage horses."[95]

The *Dallas Commercial* recounted the story in its July 25 edition:

> *We have been shown the daguerreotype likeness of Reed and of the girl he seduced about Dallas, and brought to San Antonio with him. He left her at San Marcos about the time of the stage robbery, and we learn that she has made her way back to Dallas. He lived with her here in San Antonio for several weeks, and the others were with him, immediately preceding the stage robbery. He has a wife and children, who, we believe, are somewhere about Dallas.*[96]

When news spread of the brazen robbery, Texans were stunned—Dallasites even more so, as the crime had been committed by one of their own. True, crime was rampant in the city and in the state, but heretofore, a U.S. federal mail coach had not yet been robbed. Many determined that it would be the last such robbery. The U.S. Mail agent, manager of the stage line and governor of Texas offered a combined reward of $7,000 for the capture of the culprits. Considering that they had stolen only $2,500, the message was clear: any attack on U.S. federal property would be dealt with promptly and harshly.[97]

The law interrogated Rosa McCommas when she returned to Dallas, but no charges were filed, as she had not participated directly in the holdup. Not so Jim Reed, who immediately fled the territory and his family.

Needless to say, Jim's departure was no big loss for Belle. Her husband had not only been unfaithful, but he had also been a reckless spendthrift. In addition to the stagecoach robbery near San Antonio, Reed had recently pulled off a lucrative robbery in the Indian territory in which he personally pocketed $10,000. Belle later told investigators:

> [W]*hile we were stopping on the Canadian River in the Indian Territory* [Reed] *told me that Watt Grayson a Creek Indian living on or near the Canadian River had over Thirty Thousand in gold, and that he meant to have it.*
>
> *Reed assembled a team of three, executed his plan and then sent for me. I went to them and they told me that they had accomplished their object and had the money to show for it, and they sat down upon the ground and began counting it. I saw they had a large amount of gold, they counted it and divided it in my presence.*

When the U.S. commissioner attempted to locate the money, Belle claimed, "That of the amount taken from Grayson, I know of no part that could be recovered, my said husband having spent or disposed of all that

Section of a 1937 mural at Fair Park in Dallas showing the settlement of Texas. *Library of Congress.*

he had and having left me in a destitute condition."[98] A second investigator confirmed Belle's claim:

[I] *inquired if any of the money taken could be secured and became satisfied that it had all been gambled off and otherwise spent.* [Reed] *had been seen gambling in gambling houses in this place* [Dallas] *with large sums of gold, and I learned that in one instance* [Reed's accomplice] *lost $3,000 in gold on one horse race, at another time he paid $1,500 in gold to release one of their gang from an arrest. They were all notorious for horse racing, and often lost large sums of money in that way. I am quite sure that the effects of all three of them together that I know of or could find would not bring 1,000 dollars.*[99]

Belle's concern for her husband (if, in fact, there was any) ended on August 6, 1874, when Jim Reed was gunned down resisting arrest. Jim Morris had been deputized to track Jim Reed down. It didn't take him long to find his prey, for Reed had returned to Texas just months after his brazen stage robbery. But he had not returned to make up with Belle. No, he had another scheme up his sleeves.

This time, Reed recruited the incognito special deputy to help him rob an old man in Arkansas. Morris jumped at the opportunity. As the two approached the border to Indian territory, Morris realized that he needed to act fast—he was deputized in Texas but carried no authority once they crossed the border. So, he suggested to his partner/prey that they stop for a meal at a house near the border. Reed agreed, and the two sat down at table. Morris finished first and went to check on the horses. While doing so, he told his host that he was entertaining a dangerous and wanted felon. The two then proceeded to remove Reed's pistols from the horse and then went inside to make the arrest. Reed was still at the table eating:

> *I said to Reed, "Jim, throw up your hands," he said he would do so, but ran under the table, and raised up with the table and ran towards the door with the table in advance. I shot two holes through the table. After he dropped the table I shot him in the right side. He ran his hand in his pocket to draw a cylinder as I thought. I shot at him four times, and hit him twice, once a scalping shot in the head and once in the right side.*[100]

Jim Reed was finally out of Belle's life for good. Another man—equally as unsavory—would soon take Reed's place. And then another.

There was little left for Belle in Texas. Sometime after August 1876, she sold her farm in Scyene and moved north. She appeared again in the historical record when she married Sam Starr, a Cherokee man of the Indian territory, and moved with her two children, Pearl and Eddie, to Younger's Bend in Stigler, Oklahoma—named, ironically, for Belle's Dallas acquaintance Cole Younger. She spent the next decade in her well-guarded home along the Canadian River in constant conflict with the law. Her home became a haven for outlaws, including, at one time, Frank and Jesse James. After a nine-month jail sentence in Detroit, Belle returned to her home in the Indian territory. When Sam Starr was killed in 1886 in a shootout with his cousin, U.S. Deputy Indian Marshal Frank West, Belle moved in with another Cherokee man named Bill July but quickly became single again when July was arrested for horse stealing.

Belle kept a low profile during her final three years. But her days as an outlaw—or at least her harboring of outlaws—eventually caught up with her. She was gunned down in 1889 near Eufaula, Oklahoma. The only man charged with her murder—Edgar Watson, a tenant she had kicked off her land—was acquitted when no witnesses could be found placing him at the scene of the ambush. Her case has never been solved.[101]

## Part III

# VIGILANTES AND VIXENS IN THE 1920s AND 1930s

## RETURN OF THE KLAN

The placard, cast orange by the light of a burning cross, bobbed down Main Street proclaiming its message to an awestruck crowd: "Dallas Must Be Clean." Its bearer wore white robes and a pointed hood. A thousand others like him marched along Main Street that night in May 1921, one man ten paces in front of the next. Each bore a red, white and blue cross on his left breast. One held an American flag. One held the burning cross. Many carried placards summarizing the Klan's tenets:

*"Here Yesterday. Here Today. Here Forever."*

*"Invisible Empire"*

*"All Pure White"*

*"The Guilty Must Pay"*

It was a Saturday night, and Main Street would normally have been lit by streetlights. But this night, the streetlights had all been turned off to hide the faces of the marching men—for dramatic effect. The burning cross shone that much brighter without competition. The electric company, it seemed, was behind the Klan.

"Ku Klux Blues," sheet music published in Dallas in 1921. *Beinecke Library at Yale University.*

The men marched down Main and turned, hitting Elm. They headed back toward the Majestic Theatre. All along the parade route, crowds cheered and clapped. Of course, there were many in Dallas who were not cheering. Reporters from the *Dallas Express*, a weekly Black newspaper, watched the parade that night and reported details from the event the following week. The newspaper tried to make sense of the display—what would the resurgence of the Klan mean for Dallas?[102]

The parade was a public debut for the Dallas Ku Klux Klan. Or rather a re-debut, since the Klan was an old organization, an organization that the Dallas marchers (average age thirty-seven) might have heard about from their grandfathers.[103] Of course, none of the marchers that day had grown up with the Klan. The organization had been defunct since the early 1870s, when the federal government took steps to crush it.[104]

Fifty years later, the group had been "exhumed," as one writer put it, when an Atlanta socialite named William Joseph Simmons obtained a charter for a new KKK from the State of Georgia. Simmons's resurrection of the group coincided with the release of D.W. Griffith's *Birth of a Nation*, a film so technically innovative that viewers were "thrilled out of their minds," Roger Ebert would write nearly one hundred years later. The film, which glorified the KKK as a force for good, was so popular that it was considered by many to be the "greatest American film" until the 1960s.[105]

William Joseph Simmons, reviver of the Ku Klux Klan. *Library of Congress.*

D.W. Griffith's 1915 film sparked new interest in the Ku Klux Klan. This 1930 film poster shows that the movie was still popular fifteen years after its release. *Library of Congress.*

Simmons's plan to make the KKK a much more hierarchical, profitable and pompous organization was more successful than he could have dreamed. Combined with his efforts and the popularity of *Birth of a Nation*, the KKK spread out from Atlanta, attracting millions of members across the country. At its peak of popularity in 1923–25, the Klan had from 5 to 9 million active members, who poured many millions of dollars in dues money into the organization. Dallas would turn out to be ripe recruiting grounds for the resurrected Klan. "In no other city did the Klan find a readier reception," one historian would write. The group would soon claim some 13,000 Dallas citizens among its members. The Klan was so popular in Dallas that the city could claim to have more members per capita than any other.[106]

The parade in May 1921 was a public coming-out party for Dallas's local Klan chapter, officially called Klan 66. But Dallas had already been introduced to Klan 66 by another means the month before the parade. As brazen as its downtown parade was, the newly formed Dallas chapter of the Klan had done something more brazen in April 1921. The Klan had abducted a local Black man, tortured him and disfigured him, and had kidnapped two newspaper reporters and brought them along to witness the attack. As graphic details from the assault appeared in papers around the nation, Klan 66's message rang clear: there's a new sheriff in town, and he wears a mask.[107]

The Klan's violent and conspicuous entrée into Dallas society was a calculated move by its local leader, a man who would soon climb the KKK ladder to its highest rung. That leader, a Dallas dentist named Hiram Wesley Evans, had become Klan 66's "exalted cyclops" by 1920. Evidence suggests that Evans personally led the April 1921 attack on the Black man. Evans's encouragement of and participation in violent thuggery ensured that the Klan's abduction of the man was not a one-off. Instead, the abduction would prove to be permission for more violence.

Over the course of a few months, Klan 66 would make headlines again and again for its abductions, assaults and torture. A pattern emerged—a mob of Klansmen would abduct a Dallas citizen accused of violating the Klan's mores. They would take the man to a remote location outside the city,

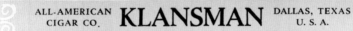

A 1923 advertisement for Dallas-based All-American Cigar Company. *Library of Congress.*

tie him up and torture and beat him. The police would prove to be rather unmotivated in the search for the perpetrators, and Dallas citizens would soon have to take matters into their own hands.

THE KLAN WAS DEAD and gone, and then it was alive again. According to the Klan itself, the resurgence of the group was a response to growing "lawlessness" in Dallas and the nation in general.

The resurgence of the Klan coincided with national Prohibition in 1920, which placed many formerly law-abiding saloon keepers, distillers and drinkers on the wrong side of the law. Two hundred saloons had operated in Dallas before Prohibition. Then, overnight, they were all shuttered. In a sixteen-month period shortly after Prohibition began, Dallas police arrested 250 men for violating liquor laws and confiscated 150 illegal stills. The Klan, a wholly Protestant Christian organization, fiercely opposed drinking and supported Prohibition.

Suddenly, Dallas had a whole lot more criminals. The Prohibition-fueled increase in the number of lawbreakers walking the streets of Dallas might have been responsible for the feeling.

One Klan proclamation, "The Guilty Must Pay," appeared on a placard at the 1921 Main Street parade. The implication was that the guilty were not paying in the Dallas of the early 1920s—the justice system was not functioning. The Klan took particular umbrage at how the judicial system functioned—they were outraged that criminals were given due process and allowed to bond out after committing crimes. To them, the guilty must pay— and swiftly. And if the justice system would not see to that, the Klan would have to. In the absence of law, the Klan would impose it, or so the rationale went. Klan 66's nighttime abductions were not examples of lawlessness, but rather a response to lawlessness—the imposition of law.[108]

It took circuitous reasoning to see the Klan's point, and some Dallasites were skeptical from the earliest days of the Klan's resurgence. The *Dallas Morning News*, an organization that would prove to be an obstinate critic of the Klan for years, decried the May Klan parade in the days afterward. The resurgence of the Klan was a "slander" on Dallas—a slander exactly because the conditions of lawlessness that the Klan had railed against did

Dallas newsboys in the early twentieth century. *Library of Congress.*

not actually exist. "Proclaiming themselves the conservators of law," the *News* wrote, "the men who marched the streets of Dallas Saturday night made themselves the exemplars of lawlessness. They seek to institute a reign of terror."[109]

Scholarship suggests that the *Dallas Morning News* may have been dead-on in its early criticism of the Klan. Dallas—and the rest of the country—did not have a problem with lawlessness. Instead, society was changing, power balances were shifting and some saw their status being diminished.

Historian Nancy MacLean explored the true causes behind the rise of the Second Ku Klux Klan in a 1994 book. As the Klan was exploding in popularity, the country was undergoing radical social change. Race riots were breaking out in cities. Women had gained the right to vote and were now wearing short skirts and smoking cigarettes. Black southerners, influenced by the newly formed NAACP, and Black veterans who had lived overseas and fought in World War I were demanding more autonomy and leaving

The Famous 369th Infantry, a unit of Black soldiers that fought in World War I, arrives in New York City circa 1918. *National Archives.*

The 1910 lynching of Allen Broooks, depicted on a postcard. *Smithsonian National Museum of African American History and Culture.*

the South in droves. The entire international order had been upended by the war. Liberal southern whites were forming groups with names like the Commission on Interracial Cooperation.

What the men who turned to the Klan for answers observed was not lawlessness but rather "instances of insubordination to old masters," MacLean wrote, "the birth pangs of a new kind of social order." Middle-class white men were finding their hands pulled farther and farther away from the levers of power. But white supremacy was still the law of the land, especially in the South. Violence against Black people was still routinely practiced—a sad fact illustrated by the infamous Dallas trial of Allen Brooks in 1910. Brooks, who had been accused of the attempted rape of a white child, was waiting in the jury room during his trial when a mob burst into the courtroom, pushed him out of a second-story window and beat him to death. His body was hanged from the imposing Elks Arch at Main and Akard Streets.

The jump to violence for frustrated middle-class white men, then, was an easy one to make.[110] The Klan's brazenness was a reflection of how much power middle-class white men still held in society—Alex Johnson's captors had little fear that law enforcement would ever hold them accountable. The Klan did not fear the law. Instead, it cast the law aside and proclaimed itself the law.

# THE ABDUCTION OF ALEX JOHNSON

Dallas was abuzz. The city was about to host a major art exhibition. The paintings, drawings and sculptures of Europe's masters would be shown at one of the city's grandest buildings: the Adolphus Hotel. The biggest names in the art world would appear signed in the corners of the works: Renoir, Cézanne, Degas, Gaugin, Monet, Matisse, Picasso and more. In all, Dallas citizens would get to admire, in person, 294 masterworks.

Although the exhibition would feature work from the most renowned of European artists, the fact that it was being held in Dallas was a sign that "it will be our turn next," wrote New York art critic Forbes Watson, who arranged the exhibition. "The bringing of such an exhibition as this to Dallas is but a sign which way the tide of art is flowing." Forbes and the Dallas Art Association hoped that the exhibition would make Dallas, just a frontier backwater fifty years before, an art beacon.[111]

Being prepared for exhibition in the hotel the night of April 1, 1921, was an oil painting by Eugene Delacroix called *Hercules and Alcestis*. In the painting, a lion skin–clad Hercules carries a swooning, bare-chested Alcestis. Hercules's gaze is fixed firmly on the woman's face, and he does not seem to notice a shadowy fiend climbing up from hell behind him. The fiend is gripping snakes in both hands and seems intent on harming Hercules. That night, six days before the opening of the exhibition, a young hotel employee would find himself caught in a perverse analogue of the painting.

The night had been going well for the employee, a Black elevator operator named Alex Johnson. He had embraced his own version of Alcestis, a white woman staying at the hotel. The two had been communing, alone in the woman's room, when fiends caught up to them. The fiends in this case would turn out to be Dallas police officers, who arrested Johnson upon learning that he was spending time alone with a white woman. Johnson spent a few hours in jail but was bonded out and allowed to go to his home on Ross Avenue.

But Johnson's troubles were only beginning. The Dallas police force in those days had been infiltrated by the Klan. The police released Johnson from custody, but it was really only a hand-off: within a few hours of his release, at around midnight, a mob of masked Klansmen—surely tipped off by and possibly including police officers—had coalesced at the Black man's house. Delacroix's fiend held snakes, and the fiends that night did too: "blacksnakes," the name for a long leather whip with a lead ball tied to one end. The whips could be used to score flesh or held upside down and used to bludgeon.

*Hercules and Alcestis,* by Ferdinand Victor Eugène Delacroix, 1862. *Phillips Collection/ Wikimedia Commons.*

The Klansmen, who numbered fifteen, forced Johnson into a car and began driving him south. Other cars followed. One made a detour to pick up two more unwilling passengers: reporters Fred D. Ball and Paul Jones. The mob wanted witnesses to the event that was about to unfold, writers who could describe in detail what the mob was about to do. Witnesses would be crucial if maximum terror was to be inflicted. The two reporters were blindfolded and forced into a car.

The Klansmen traveled for six miles, well past the limits of the city, to the bottoms of the Trinity River near present-day Hutchins, Texas. When the car carrying the reporters stopped, the two men were pulled out into the quiet of the country night. Their blindfolds were "snatched" off their faces, and their eyes beheld a terrible sight: Alex Johnson stood beneath what would soon be known as the "Torture Tree," with a gang of well-dressed but masked men standing around him. Around Johnson's neck was fastened a rope.[112] He was cast yellow by the light of a flashlight bulb.

The Klansmen who surrounded him had played at being police officers when they arrested, bound and transported Johnson. Now they would play at being judges, jurors and executioners. If the Klan was going to take the law into its hands, why not take the entire judicial process? The men pantomimed a trial, examining the man as he begged for his life. What is your name? What do you do for a living? What happens after dark at the Adolphus Hotel?

The men questioned Johnson "coolly and methodically," Ball and Jones would report. The Klansmen let Johnson know that they were considering imposing the death sentence. Johnson, terrified, "confessed." He had been officially charged with vagrancy, an ambiguous accusation usually directed at the jobless, homeless or transient. But the ambiguous nature of the crime allowed it to be used against someone like Johnson, who had a job and a home—both facts mentioned in the report of his abduction.

In early twentieth-century America, vagrancy charges were, as one scholar put it, a means of "social control that criminalizes certain populations in order to facilitate selective punishment"—in other words, a way to legally punish someone who had not clearly broken a law. Vagrancy was a crime of "being," rather than a crime of "acting."

Under a Texas statute of the era, prostitutes were legally considered vagrants. Some have suggested that Johnson might have been sleeping with a white prostitute when he was arrested. The official crackdown on vice in the early twentieth century had pushed much illegal drinking and sex into hotels. Hotel bellboys found themselves natural middlemen, earning a "virtual monopoly" on hotel-based prostitution, one historian wrote.[113]

A street scene in 1913 Dallas. *Library of Congress.*

Johnson admitted (under extreme duress) to having sex with the white woman but swore that it had been consensual. Johnson gave the Klansmen other details about what went on generally at the Adolphus Hotel, but the newspaper report gave no details, only mentioning that Johnson had told a "sordid story of night life at the hotel."

The Klan members finished their deposition of Johnson with a final question: "If we spare your life, will you ever commit such an offense as this again?"

"God help me, no," Johnson replied.

The Klansmen stripped Johnson's shirt and jacket, led him to a fence and tied him. Each member of the mob took a turn lashing his back with the blacksnake. "Each lash tore a bit of skin from the naked black's back," the reporters related to readers soon after.

The mobbed whipped Johnson twenty-five times, but still his ordeal was not over. One of the Klansmen took a small bottle from his pocket, explaining to Ball that it was silver nitrate, a chemical used to develop film. The Klansman dipped a brush into the bottle and carefully painted the letters "K.K.K." on Johnson's forehead. Then they attached a padlock to the man, forced him back into one of the cars, drove him back to Dallas and dropped him off in front of the Adolphus Hotel.

The official police response to the abduction was a preview of the police inaction that would follow in the coming months. The Associated Press reported that no police action had taken place the day after Johnson was dropped off, a "bleeding mass of stripes and welts," in downtown Dallas—and that no police action was expected. City officials claimed that since the beating had taken place outside city limits, they had no jurisdiction in the case. The Dallas County sheriff was more blunt, saying that Johnson "was guilty of consorting with a white woman and that the beating was no more than he deserved."[114]

As news of more abductions spread in the press, the police again and again reported that they had no leads in the cases, always mentioning that no evidence pointed to Ku Klux Klan involvement.

## THE WIZARD OF DALLAS

The goblin was supposed to keep his mouth shut. Now here he was, spilling the beans about Dallas's most enthusiastic proponent of "rough stuff"—the torture required of Dallas Klansmen when nothing else would do. The man testifying in the Harris County, Texas courthouse that fall day in 1923 was George B. Kimbro Jr., a Klan business manager for nine states who held the official title "Grand Goblin." Kimbro had been uneasy with the violence used so freely by some in his organization, and two years after the abduction of Alex Johnson, he testified against his associates in court. His testimony revealed the names of the men who had committed violence with their faces obscured by masks. It was an update to newspaper stories that had appeared years before, including the story about Alex Johnson's abduction and torture.

Key details from the crime emerged, including the names of Bertram Christie, the founder of Klan 66; George Butcher, a businessman who would go on to become an officer of Klan 66; and Hiram Wesley Evans, who would soon become infamous well outside the city limits of Dallas.

Evans—a stout, businesslike man who suffered bouts of lumbago—had been born in Alabama but had made his way to Nashville as a young man, where he studied at Vanderbilt. He didn't earn a degree (and in fact the university has no record of him ever being admitted), but the education he received there enabled him to move to Dallas around 1900 and begin practicing dentistry.

He ran a small practice, catering to Black patients. He had lived and worked in the city for two decades and was facing his fortieth year in 1920 when Dallas got its own branch of the Klan. It was just what he'd been looking for. Evans joined, a charter member.

Within a year of joining, Evans had replaced Christie as Klan 66's "Exalted Cyclops," the chapter's highest-ranking local member. It was under his direction that the Klan took Alex Johnson from his home and flogged him in April 1921. Evans had not only ordered the abduction, but he had also participated himself—details made public by Kimbro's testimony.[115]

When Kimbro had pled with Evans to stop the violence, Evans had "fought" him, using his own history of participation in the abductions as supporting evidence of why they should continue. It's likely that Evans's leadership is a major reason why Dallas developed such an active Klan presence and why so many reports of abduction and torture came from the city. In the span of a year, at least sixty-five men were abducted and taken to the Torture Tree.[116]

Another former associate of Evans, Judge Erwin J. Clark, who had been a Klan leader in Waco, testified before a U.S. Senate subcommittee in 1924, further illuminating Evans's mind-set at the time he was coordinating abductions in the city. Clark described a man who not only masterminded attacks but also sought to parlay the fear generated by those attacks into

Hiram Wesley Evans marching in a Klan parade in Washington, D.C. *Library of Congress.*

political victories. The Dallas Klan would prove to be so effective a political machine that it would sweep local elections in 1922, electing eighteen of nineteen Klan-backed candidates to local office.[117]

Evans considered the Klan in Texas to be a "great militant political organization" and its "militancy" to be an essential characteristic if it were to survive. Judge Clark recalled telling Evans that even the Ku Klux Klan might be too democratically minded to tolerate the level of militancy Evans thought necessary.

Clark recalled a conversation he had had with Evans and other Texas Klan leaders about a year after Alex Johnson's abduction. By that time, Evans had already risen to a higher rank in the national Klan organization and was no longer the leader in Dallas. The Dallas papers had been "full of tar and feathers and flogging parties that had been held at Dallas," Clark had told Evans. Evans feigned outrage, saying that he would travel back to Dallas and put a stop to the attacks. His companions laughed and told him to stop being a hypocrite—they remembered that he had led the attack on Johnson just a year before. Rebuffed, Evans silently paced the floor, while another of the leaders present, H.C. McCall of Houston, expounded on why it was essential that the violence continue. "The best way to put the fear of god into the negroes [is] to take them out and work them over occasionally," McCall told his companions. "If we did not do that the negroes might attempt to dominate our primaries."[118]

Evans's feigned outrage in front of his fellow Klan leaders just a year after personally directing attacks in Dallas was a sign that he might be rethinking the expedience of Klan violence. Leaders within the organization were disturbed by the violence and called for it to stop, and that was nothing compared to public condemnation the Klan attacks were beginning to draw.

Publications in Dallas—foremost among them the *Dallas Morning News*—had been vocally critical of the Klan since it re-formed. But the year of abductions and terror in Dallas had galvanized ordinary citizens as well. In March 1922, a mass meeting of Dallas citizens was called by a group of multidenominational business and church leaders to "consider means of putting an end to the series of whippings of Dallas men by masked and unmasked bands." The meeting turned out to be immensely popular—five thousand people showed up at the city auditorium and agreed to form the Dallas County Citizens League, a group whose express purpose would be to exorcise the Ku Klux Klan from public office in Dallas.[119]

Evans, who had found his vehicle out of a middling existence as a dentist, would do anything possible to ensure that he continued rising through Klan ranks, even if that meant joining the public outcry for a stop to Klan violence. Within two years of joining the Klan, Evans had risen from member to local leader, regional leader and national secretary. In November 1922, he achieved the ultimate prize: the Imperial Wizardship. The Dallas dentist who not long ago had catered to Black customers was now the leader of the national Ku Klux Klan. Ironically, one of the first things Evans would do as national leader was denounce any chapter that engaged in violence. He outlawed the use of robes, hoods and masks except for during official Klan functions—parades, meetings and church visits. His about-face on the Klan's use of violence was purely practical—Evans had decided that the violence brought too much negative press, that the damage to the Klan's political power outweighed the benefits. Evans's decrees essentially ended Klan vigilantism.[120]

Evans's pivot could not undo the harm a year of night-riding had done to the Klan's reputation in Dallas. The Dallas County Citizens League, along with other similar-minded groups across Texas, threw their support behind anti-Klan gubernatorial candidate Miriam Ferguson in the 1924 Texas gubernatorial race. Ferguson's opponent in the Democratic primary was Dallas judge Felix D. Robertson, a Klansman himself. Dallas voted overwhelmingly for Robertson, but he couldn't beat Ferguson statewide. Ferguson went on to become governor. The Texas legislature passed an anti-mask law that criminalized wearing a mask in public or committing crimes or parading while masked.

A demoralized Dallas Klan quickly succumbed to infighting and financial mismanagement, in two years losing some 92 percent of its membership. By 1926, there were only 1,200 active Klansmen in Dallas. The Texas Klan more generally suffered similar losses.

Dallas's latter-day Klansmen had cast law and order aside in pursuit of law and order. But Dallas's citizens, and Texans more generally, had seen the corruption of their reasoning and rejected vigilantism. The hopeful art lovers who had organized Dallas's exhibition of European masters must have felt demoralized when the Klan chose the Adolphus Hotel as the launching point for their campaign of terror. But the eventual rejection of Klan violence by the citizens of Dallas and Texas showed that decency would triumph in the end.

## THE "SLAYRESS" OF DEEP ELLUM

*I told her I loved her man,*
*grave will be her resting place.*
*(Repeat)*
*She looked at me with burning eyes,*
*threw carbolic acid in my face.*
*In my bed, my face burned to the bone.*
*(Repeat)*
*If carbolic don't kill me,*
*penitentiary gonna be my home.*[121]

The Dallas skyline in the first decades of the twentieth century. *Library of Congress.*

Crime in Dallas is generally associated with the red-blooded males of the city. Brawling, pimping, gambling and killing were traditionally male pastimes. And the music that encouraged such behavior—blues, the "Devil's Music"—was played by men. And yet a handful of women in 1920s and '30s Dallas were determined to prove that stereotype wrong.

W.E. KING WAS WAITING for his evening meal. It was 2:30 p.m. and he was hungry. He hadn't expended much energy over the last few weeks, and he didn't necessarily need the calories. But there was little else to do. Truth be told, W.E. was bored. Ever since he fell off that streetcar, he'd been convalescing at home. He was ready to be healthy again, ready to start moving about the city again. A few more hot lunches and a few more restful nights and he would be out and about again. His housekeeper was fixing him a meal in the kitchen when he heard the knock at the door.

SHE HAD A PLAN. The .38-caliber pistol in her purse would help her execute it—and execute him. Hattie Burleson got out of her friend's car at 2811 Flora Street. She shut the car door and it drove out of sight. Hattie then began walking toward the house.

W.E. KING WAS GOING to get a good lunch. He almost always did. His housekeeper was a good cook, and she knew it. Another dozen or so of her meals and he would be as good as new. The food was nearly ready when she heard a guest knock and enter. Moments later, she realized it

was a woman when she heard an impassioned argument erupt in the other room. Mr. King and the mystery woman quickly began shouting at each other.

He was not going to let some damn secretary raise her voice at him. He was William Elisha King, one of the most prominent Black men in Dallas. He was the founder and editor of the popular *Dallas Express*. And now this young secretary stood in front of him, yelling at him as if he were common trash.

W.E. King was not going to be intimidated. He had been born and raised and became a man in Mississippi—and in 1870s and 1880s Mississippi at that. Born the year after the Civil War ended and just entering an early adulthood when the state was "redeemed" by white, racist Democrats, King knew danger when he saw it. He had already been forced to flee one state, to shut down one paper, to be silent in order to live.

He had vowed he would not be silenced again. He moved to Dallas and began a paper with the goal of educating his own community. His paper was a success, and he was soon in great demand as a lecturer. He pursued both vocations—public speaker and public writer—with great passion. Through hard work and courage, lots of courage, he had become an exemplar of his race.

And now this woman dared stand there and shout at him in his own home.

HOW DARE HE RAISE his voice to her. After all she had given him— professionally and personally, at the office and in that very house. Didn't he know who she was? She had been a secretary, but now she was a businesswoman. She ran a rooming house on the same block as his newspaper office. And her ambitions soared much higher than that. She

Mural in present-day Deep Ellum. *Library of Congress.*

knew she had a talent. One day soon, everyone else would realize that too. Today, everyone knew the name W.E. King. Tomorrow, everyone would know the name Hattie Burleson. His name was on the masthead of every newspaper he published. Hers would be in bright lights.

THE SHOUTING CONTINUED TO escalate. And then, *bang!* It stopped. Terrified, the housekeeper nevertheless ran into the room. The woman was walking out the front door. Mr. King lay on the floor, an expanding puddle of blood beneath him.

Moments later, Dr. Roy O. Busch arrived. He saw the hole in King's chest and knew it had been a fatal shot. The doctor did what he could and watched as the most famous Black man in Dallas died of a gunshot wound on the floor of his own house.

Hattie Burleson calmly walked down nearby Cochran Street. When she got to the high school, a car pulled up; she got in and had the driver take her to her house. Moments later, she walked back outside wearing a fresh change of clothes, leaving her bloodied outfit behind. Her driver then drove her to the police station, where Hattie Burleson surrendered to the authorities.[122]

A little more than a month later, a grand jury exonerated her, and Hattie Burleson walked away a free woman.[123] Hattie returned to her career in the joints and theaters of Deep Ellum. The 1920s and 1930s provided ample opportunity in this mecca of Dallas entertainment. A large number of Jews opened their businesses along Deep Ellum and Central Track (historically a Black neighborhood)—most notably the pawnshop, the staple of Deep Ellum. Herschel Wilonsky, the son of a shop owner who lived and worked on Elm Street, recalled:

*Probably the liveliest place in the city of Dallas was Deep Ellum. That was the most busy place you'd ever see. Looking back at it now, it was kind of like a city sidewalk in New York at 12:30 in the afternoon. On whatever street you're walking up, people just walking into you. That's what Deep Ellum was. Everything happened, I mean nightclubs, black nightclubs, white nightclubs. The place was hopping. You could go downtown any night of the week.[124]*

Illustration based on a drawing of the "Nile Queen," featured in an ad for hair products that ran in the *Dallas Express* at the time its editor was killed. *Josh Foreman.*

Judith gloats over the severed head of Holofernes. Barthel Beham, 1525. *Rijksmuseum.*

Black musician Sammy Price remembered, "In Deep Ellum, there was an alley called 'death row,' where someone would get killed every Saturday."[125] Jewish pawnbroker "Rocky" Goldstein confirmed Price's claim: "There was a killing every day. There were fights on the corner of Central and Elm all the time, and they had these Holy-Roller women trying to convert these guys."[126]

Deep Ellum was certainly a lively district, exactly the place where a "slayress" would feel at home. It was a city within a city full of businessmen, hustlers, entertainers, prostitutes and murderers. It was also a vital symbol of what Dallas had been since its founding: a perpetual contradiction, a city of prestige and promise and wealth but also destitution, despair and violence. Alan Govenar and Jay Brakefield summed up Deep Ellum of the 1920s and 1930s:

> *It was a business district that became legendary for violence and sin. As the song "Deep Ellum Blues" says, one went "down" on or in Deep Ellum, down to a world where people broke the accepted norms of behavior. Deep Ellum was a real place that provided a variety of services, legal and illegal, and came to represent the uncertainties and dangers associated with the growth of Dallas as a city.*[127]

Deep Ellum was "the other side of Dallas," the side where mostly Black and some Jewish citizens resided, where entertainment and business and crime existed side by side. And yet poverty and crime were not "Black" or "Jewish" problems, for there were white sections of Dallas with a parallel history. Had they been capable of empathy in that Jim Crow era, many marginalized whites in Dallas would have identified with their segregated brethren and seen the common result of poverty and hopelessness.

## BONNIE PARKER: WEST DALLAS GIRL

She was destined to be a star. She was sure of it. So was her mother. From birth on, Bonnie was the darling of her family, the darling of her community and, for a time, America's darling—albeit a sexy, forbidden siren with a dark side. In 1924, at age fourteen, she was just a darling.

Bonnie was raised in poverty. She had the ambition but never the means to give her dreams an honest chance. The one thing she did have undisputed

Bonnie Parker as depicted in *Crime Does Not Pay*, no. 57, 1946–47. *Internet Archive.*

access to was boys. And they didn't cost anything. In fact, if she played it right, they could prove to be quite profitable.

For Bonnie, "playing it right" was never a problem. She had always been a fashionista. She knew how to work the long, slenderizing skirts and jersey tops; the eyeliner, rouge and lipstick; and the berets and short permed hair.[128] And she had the moxie. Bonnie never lacked for confidence. When her sister tried to hush her singing one day, Bonnie retorted, "When I'm on Broadway and I have my name in lights, you'll be sorry you talked to me like this." While her friends went to Fair Park to take three-for-a-nickel photographs, Bonnie saved her money and had fancy glamour shots done in an actual studio.

Her cousin Bess remembered that Bonnie "had a lot of 'fellers' in grade school—boys who thought she was too cute for anything. Bonnie always had a book satchel full of candy bars, chewing gum and sort of mashed looking apples that some little boy had brought her."[129]

One of Bonnie's earliest beaus was a boy named Noel. The smitten Noel bought ten-year-old Bonnie whatever he could afford. One day, however, he did something to make his girl angry—real angry. Bonnie chased him down the street and began to pummel him in front of the local drugstore. Finally, a passerby dragged Bonnie off Noel. She was horrified to find that Bonnie was holding a razor blade and threatening to cut Noel's throat if he ever angered her again.[130]

But Bonnie had a sweet side too. In fact, to many she was irresistible. She was a vivacious conversationalist. She had a spunky personality. She lived on the edge, and much of the nation—especially the poor and marginalized—would one day live vicariously through her. But the bottom line was she was just so damn cute and likeable.

WEST DALLAS OF THE 1910s and 1920s was "the bastard stepchild of the city of Dallas."[131] It's where people ended up when they had nowhere else to go. It's where those forced to leave their farms due to a nonexistent cotton market hunkered down. It's where a number of Dallas's most notorious criminals were spawned.

Less than 10 percent of West Dallas homes had indoor plumbing in the years immediately following World War I. About as many had electricity. The houses were made of whatever materials could be scavenged from the local dump. Some simply lived under the wagons they brought with them when they were evicted from their farms. The roads were unpaved (with the sole exception of Eagle Ford Road), and what few street signs that were posted were torn down by inhabitants who did not want to be located. Not surprisingly, West Dallas became a breeding ground for despair and crime.[132]

LIKE MOST RESIDENTS OF West Dallas, Bonnie wanted out. There were very few amusements for a promising and attractive girl in West Dallas. Of course, there was always Dallas proper, whose skyscrapers basically cast shadows on West Dallas. But those amusements cost money—something few in West Dallas could spare. Nevertheless, when Bonnie did have some rare spare change, she hopped on over to the wealthier side of town, where she would indulge in an occasional movie, have her picture taken at the manifold picture booths or maybe grab a bite to eat.

Bonnie was a typical teenager in that she craved companionship, activity and adventure—something to do. "Not a thing helps out though. Sure am blue. Everything has gone wrong today. Why don't something happen? What a life!"[133] Popular as she was, Bonnie could never seem to satisfy the longing deep down inside her for adventure—nor for love.

One day soon, Bonnie's loneliness and restlessness would be eased, somewhat, by a small, sharp-dressed, fast-moving man. And then her problems would really begin.

WHEN BONNIE WASN'T WITH a beau, she often found solace in one of the myriad movie theaters in town. Almost as soon as movies became available to the masses, Dallasites fell in love with the pastime. By the end of the Second World War, Dallas had become the "Amusement capital of the Southwest."[134] Unfortunately for Bonnie, she would not be around to see the rapid growth of one of her favorite pastimes. Nor would she have the opportunity to view such shows during her final years, although she would unknowingly become the star of quite a few, posthumously.

Bonnie enjoyed movies where a handsome man was in charge. One of her favorites was *The Night of Love,* where Ronald Colman plays a man whose young bride dies after she is kidnapped and nearly raped. Colman swears to avenge his beloved. Here was a man who understood love—one who would fight (and kill) for his beloved.[135]

Bonnie kept a diary for about two weeks, and in that brief time, she went to seven movies. "This is New Year's Day, January 1. I went to a show. Saw Ken Maynard in 'The Overland Stage.'"[136] "Met Rosa Mary today and we went to a show. Saw Ronald Colman and Vilma Banky in 'A Night of Love.' Sure was a good show."[137] "Well, I went down town today and saw a picture. Milton Sills in 'Framed.' Sure was a good picture."[138]

Bonnie adored the actresses on screen, and she longed for their onscreen lovers. She craved adventure and love; she had little of either. The movies became her surrogate.

A single girl had to support herself. And there just weren't that many options for a young girl from the wrong side of Dallas. Now, Bonnie was smart. In fact, she excelled in school. But it didn't matter. She might as well have dropped out after grade school. Like her fellow West Dallasites, college was not an option; there simply wasn't any money. Bonnie could be a factory line worker, a maid, a waitress or a clerk.[139] And then there were the more illicit means of earning a living. A pretty, flirtatious girl like Bonnie would have no trouble finding customers.

There is no proof that Bonnie ever actually engaged in prostitution. She did, however, have a very keen understanding of how the system worked in West Dallas. One of her poems, "The Prostitutes' Convention,"[140] is a detailed list of which West Dallas girls were turning tricks and on what street corners. She certainly was familiar with the age-old practice. And she was pretty and charming enough to make some money to supplement her income as a waitress if she so chose.[141]

More likely, Bonnie was just in love with being in love, intent on finding a Prince Charming, a Ronald Colman or Milton Sills to sweep her off her feet. Just like they did in the movies. Bonnie always had "fellers" and "sweethearts"—boys who couldn't help but give her pencils and candies and goodies—but she didn't start going on actual dates until she was fifteen.[142] Shortly thereafter, she was in love.

Roy Thornton was tall, suave and good looking. He made decent money, at least by West Dallas standards. He liked to have fun and had the money to do so. He moved with a fast crowd. Bonnie knew that she had met her Prince. Soon after meeting Roy, Bonnie had two hearts connected by arrows tattooed into the inside of her thigh. They read "Roy" and "Bonnie."

Bonnie's mother, Emma, resisted. Sure, Roy was a nice catch—just not for her daughter, for whom she had such high hopes. But the headstrong, heart-strong Bonnie was not going to be told no. She was in love. Love was forever. Love couldn't wait.

The two were married, with Emma's eventual blessing—few could resist the pleas of a weeping Bonnie—on September 25, 1926, two weeks before Bonnie turned sixteen. It was supposed to be happily ever after forever.[143] Fifteen months later, she began a diary with the following entry:

> *Before opening this year's diary, I wish to tell you that I have a roaming husband with a roaming mind. We are separated again for the third and last time....I love him very much and miss him terribly. But I intend doing my duty. I am not going to take him back....Let all men go to hell!*[144]

The marriage of Bonnie and Roy, in fact, did last forever—they just didn't live together for more than a year at a time. Roy paid the bills but wouldn't tell Bonnie how. That was okay, as long as he took her out and kept her in style. But then he started staying out all night. Then for ten days at a time. Then twenty. Then for a year.

Bonnie was furious, lonesome and depressed. "Am very blue. Well, I must confess this New Year's nite I got drunk. Trying to forget. Drowning my sorrows in bottled hell."[145] "Came home at 5:30. Went to bed at 10:30. Sure am lonesome."[146] Roy's absence began to take its toll on Bonnie. She needed to be loved, and she needed to love. She couldn't survive without action and passion in her life. With Roy gone, she began to look for love elsewhere, but nothing could fill the emptiness inside her:

> *Saw Scottie and gave him the air. He's a pain in the neck to me.*[147]... *Tonight I went with Lewis again. Not a darn thing to do. I met Johnnie Baker tonite for the first time in a long time. Still the same old Johnnie. But I don't care anything about him. Roy is always in my mind....Oh, god, how I wish I could see Roy! But I try my best to brush all thought of him aside and have a good time. If I knew for sure he didn't care for me, I'd cut my throat and say here goes nothing.*[148]...*I went with Lewis and Fred but I can't have a good time. I love my husband. I always think of him. If God would only let me find where he is.*[149]

Finally, one year later, Roy returned to Bonnie, but it was too late. Her passionate love for her husband had burned out over the course of twelve months of abandonment. She told Roy to leave, and she never saw him again. And yet, she always wore the wedding ring he had bought her on her finger and kept his name ensconced in a tattooed heart on her thigh. She never filed for divorce. Bonnie Parker died Bonnie Thornton.

Roy Thornton spent the next eight years, his last eight years, in and out of prison. He was finally killed in October 1937 while trying to escape from Eastham Prison. He outlived his estranged bride by only a few years.[150]

## BONNIE MEETS CLYDE

With Roy in prison, Bonnie would have been free to pursue her true love, to find a man to love her as she deserved. But in order to remarry, she had to first divorce him. And she wouldn't. She continued to go out with boys but seemed to have grown jaded with love. Her mother, Emma, explained: "She had beaus—she always had beaus—and went about to dances now and then, or to shows. But she made no effort to get a divorce, and when I asked her why, she said: 'Well, I didn't get it before Roy was sent up, and it looks sort of dirty to file for one now. Besides, I don't want to marry anybody else, so I'll just wait, mama.'"[151] That was that—Bonnie was finished with love.

And then she met the love of her life, the man who would teach her the literal meaning of "'Til death do us part."

Bonnie attended a house party on a fateful evening in 1930. There she met a dapper man who immediately caught her eye. The two talked, and Bonnie quickly knew that she had found her Mr. Right. She took her new man almost immediately to meet her mother, who would later recall that he "was a likeable boy…with his dark wavy hair, dancing brown eyes and a dimple that popped out every now and then when he smiled." Emma Parker saw that her daughter was definitely over Roy. "She never worshipped him as she did [her new beau]."[152]

Emma would later come to rue the day her precious girl met this charming and dangerous young man, and she would try several times to convince her to leave him.

From then on, Bonnie and her beau were inseparable—except when he was in prison, which he often was. When he was free, he was good to her—in spite of the times they fought violently. He would take her out to eat and buy her jewelry and clothes—with money he had stolen. Dora Goldstein, who ran a pawnshop in Deep Ellum, recalled the early 1930s, when Bonnie's man would take her shopping and buy her dresses: "They were just a couple of kids in love."[153] Soon they would be a couple of murderers on the run.

BONNIE SAT ON THE ground playing with Sonny Boy, a bunny she planned to give to her mother as an Easter present. Bonnie was looking forward to the visit. She had not seen much of her mother over the past two years, and the few visits had been brief. These extended absences were out of character for Bonnie. She was a devoted daughter, perhaps fanatically so. (Immediately after marrying Roy, she insisted on visiting her mother every night. It got to the point where Emma told Roy that they better just move in with her; they did.)[154] But the devoted daughter had been traveling quite a bit lately. She and her lover had been to Michigan, Iowa, Missouri, Arkansas, Oklahoma, Mississippi and Louisiana. They had become celebrities, adored by much of the American public—just as Bonnie had always expected. Her name wasn't in bright lights, as she had always promised, but rather in large, bold headlines in newspapers and magazines across the country.

Everybody who saw or read about her wanted her or wanted to be her. Boys fantasized about being with the lithe, sexy, cigar-smoking vixen. Girls wanted the true, perfect love she had found—destined to elude and overcome all obstacles. And the police wanted her in the electric chair for a plethora of robberies and murders.

Now she sat in a field, just outside of Dallas, on Texas Highway 114, playing with her bunny, awaiting the arrival of her mother. Her boyfriend was taking a nap in their stolen black Ford V-8 sedan. A third man, Henry Methvin, had joined the two lovers two months ago when Bonnie and her man had broken some friends out of Eastham Prison. Henry was not the one they were hoping to free, but he leaped into their getaway car nonetheless and had been with them ever since. He was now passing the time drinking. Bonnie kept him company, and the two passed the whiskey bottle back and forth.

Bonnie had taken to drinking over the last year. Nine months ago, she had been in a serious car wreck, and her right leg had been burned by battery acid so badly that sections of her leg bone had been visible. She would spend the rest of her life with a debilitating limp,[155] oftentimes relying on her boyfriend (who likewise walked with a limp, having cut off two of his toes to get out of the fields while he served time in Eastham Prison)[156] to carry her to and from the cars that so often served as their hotels while they ran from the "laws." And then there was that time in Platte City, Missouri, when she watched her boyfriend's brother have his brain exposed by a bullet while a glass windshield exploded into his wife's eyes as she tried to cover his body with her own.[157] And there was the shootout at Dexfield Park in Iowa when several shotgun pellets penetrated her abdomen as they ran from yet another ambush.[158] And the time they were surprised as they pulled up to meet her mother and a BAR slug went through both their legs as they sped away.[159] And all the narrow escapes and harrowing chases since. The alcohol helped.

Today, she drank until her mind was eased enough to nap. Bonnie knew that her mother would arrive later that afternoon, so just before she dozed off, she chewed on some lemon slices. She began eating lemons religiously about the time she began drinking. She was, after all, a fashionable lady. The lemons masked the booze on her breath. And she certainly didn't want her mother to know about her increasing alcohol consumption.

Henry, however, stayed awake. He immediately alerted the napping lovers when he saw two police officers approach on motorcycle. As one officer dismounted, Henry raised his rifle and shot one, killing him instantly. Bonnie's boyfriend took care of the other, knocking him off his motorcycle with a shotgun blast. Henry then walked over and shot the fallen cop several more times. The three of them, accompanied by Sonny Boy, then sped off in their Ford V8.[160]

Seven weeks later, on May 23, 1934, Bonnie and Clyde would be killed in an ambush while driving on a road in Bienville Parish, Louisiana. Bonnie was shot twenty-six times. She died the celebrity she always knew she would be. Her gravestone at Crown Hill Memorial Park in Dallas, Texas, reads:

*As the flowers are all made sweeter by the sunshine and the dew, so this old world is made brighter by the lives of folks like you.*[161]

The thirteen people killed by Bonnie and her beau would strongly disagree.

## POOR HORSEMEN, PART I: TOXIC LOVE BLOSSOMS IN DALLAS

Acie Coffman had it all. But he wanted more. Coffman, who went by "Brooks," had begun his life in Panola County, Mississippi, the son of two farmers who longed to move west. His parents fulfilled their ambition, leaving the hills of north Mississippi for prairieland 450 miles southwest in Collin County, Texas. There his father practiced politics and cultivated influence.

Brooks had gone to public school in Royse City, a tiny town about thirty miles outside Dallas that had only existed for a few decades. Growing into adulthood, Brooks showed an interest in higher education and enrolled at the newly formed Burleson College in nearby Greenville, Texas. But home called him back, and after studying at Burleson, he returned to Collin County. It seemed like he would stay in the town and pursue a modest life as a husband, father and restaurateur. He married Myrtle Stimson, a Collin County local, when he was just nineteen. They immediately started a family, with Myrtle giving birth to a son, Billie.

Brooks and his wife spent a few years in Royse City working and raising their son. But Myrtle wanted more for her husband. He wanted more too. Dallas beckoned. They decided to move to the city in the early 1920s. The 1924 Dallas City Directory shows the couple living on Annex Avenue in the northeast part of the city and Brooks employed as a salesman. Within a few years, he had found a federal job as a collector with the Bureau of Internal Revenue.

Brooks had a stable job, one that would provide employment at a time when many others were struggling to make ends meet. But with the Great Depression in full swing, Brooks decided that he had not yet attained all he wanted. Perhaps influenced by his brother John D. Coffman, who had become the assistant district attorney for Dallas County, he saw the legal practice as a means of ascending. He resolved to study law at night and take the Texas bar exam.[162]

It happened that another young Dallas citizen of the time was interested in studying law too. She was a colleague of Brooks's at the Bureau of Internal Revenue. She would express an interest in the law but a deeper interest in Brooks Coffman himself. Her name was Corinne Maddox.

When Brooks met Corinne, he was a man of thirty-four. She was only twenty—practically still a girl. But she had already endured hardship in her short life. Her parents' marriage was on the rocks, and Corinne had spent her high school years living in a house on Hollywood Avenue with her mother, aunt, sister and cousin. Corinne had been a member of the Travelers Club in high school—she had longed to leave the confines of Dallas. And she did, eloping to Oklahoma with a high school classmate, John Goswick, when she was just seventeen. The young couple soon returned to Dallas. Corinne found work as a stenographer at the Bureau of Internal Revenue. The couple realized their marriage had been a mistake. Their union was not a happy one.[163]

*Left*: Brooks Coffman. *Josh Foreman. Right*: Corinne Maddox in her 1931 Sunset High School yearbook. *Sunset High School/Ancestry.com.*

Although in his thirties, Brooks Coffman still had his looks. He had a sharp jawline, a broad nose and big gray eyes. His hairline was receding, but he still had plenty of thick black hair left. He combed it straight back. He had a lean, sharp look—years had not brought softness to his features. He was not only handsome, an account from the time reported, but debonair too.

Corinne's 1931 yearbook photo from Sunset High School shows a girl with sharp eyes, a round face and a half smile. Her blond hair is cut into a bob, the fashionable style of the time. She wears a jacket with wide lapels and two pearl necklaces. Her gaze, posture and clothes suggest she is a serious, ambitious girl. A newspaper account from a few years later would describe her as "much younger than his wife—and much more beautiful, with her wide blue eyes, her golden hair, her pert nose, and her ready smile."[164]

The same newspaper account would suggest that Brooks and Corinne's affair had begun "casually enough," with Brooks offering to drive the twenty-year-old home after work. It might have begun casually, but it had also begun intentionally. Brooks Coffman knew what he was doing. As details of the couple's relationship appeared in newspapers around the country in coming years, it would become clear that Brooks had a vice: women.

She accepted Brooks's offer and soon became a regular passenger in his car. Brooks began getting to know the girl, telling her about his family and his ambitions. "I'm going to be a lawyer," he told Corinne.

"You are! Gee, I wish I could be one," she replied. "But I'm not smart enough."

Brooks reassured the girl, "Sure you are. Why don't you study with me?"

They began studying together at night. Brooks passed the bar exam at Austin. He became a lawyer and continued tutoring Corinne. She asked him for help with another matter too—she was still legally married. Could he help her get a divorce? He agreed, and soon she was legally split from her husband, whom she accused of being "harsh, cruel, and inhuman." Corinne had a tutor, a helper and a hero—an attractive older man whose life trajectory pointed upward.

Corinne's divorce left her officially single. But the man she was falling for was not. Brooks Coffman had always wanted more, and now he found himself in a position to reach for more—for more variety of sexual experience, for more female attention, for more clandestine excitement. He decided that Corinne could provide what he had been searching for. He began to drive the young woman to motels and an abandoned gravel pit on the outskirts of town. And he would continue to live with his wife and two children for the next six years, continue to go to his wife for sex when Corinne did not sate him, continue to grow his family.

All along, Corinne Maddox would wonder what the future held for her and Brooks Coffman. Could she ever be his partner? Should she even try? Or was she destined to be his mistress, a side dish for a man with a large appetite? Was she in control of her own destiny?

In the end, Brooks would realize, as Corinne stood over him as his blood soaked into the concrete of a Dallas sidewalk, that perhaps his appetite had been too great. Perhaps he should have been content with a family, a wife and kids and a discreet mistress. But it would be far too late at that moment to change anything. Acie Brooks Coffman would realize, in the final moments of his life, that he had asked for too much from Corinne Maddox.

## POOR HORSEMEN, PART II: A BLOSSOM BEGINS TO ROT

When Wall Street share prices crashed in October 1929, sending the nation into the Great Depression, Dallas leaders were confident that the city would not be hit as hard as others. Dallas was not "in the path of the tornado that hit the exchanges" and "will suffer little direct bad effect," the business editor of the *Dallas Morning News* wrote a few days after the crash. It only took a few months for everyone to realize that Dallas would be hit just as hard as everyone else. The prices of oil and cotton, two of Dallas's most important commodities, fell hard. By 1931, the city had 18,500 unemployed workers.

Public and private organizations sprang into action, launching a host of initiatives to help alleviate the effects of the Depression. Although cotton was cheap, clothing was in short supply. Tens of thousands of garments made from government cloth were distributed to needy families via the Red Cross and other organizations. The Adolphus Hotel opened a "sewing room" where volunteers cut and sewed clothing for the relief effort. The Salvation Army provided shelter and food for women and children whose husbands had lost their jobs. Sanger's Department Store downtown hosted talent competitions for local schoolkids and awarded cash prizes to winners.[165]

City officials dealt with the Depression with a combination of belt-tightening and make-work programs. Guided by a conservative fiscal policy

A farmer outside Dallas. Photo by Dorothea Lange, 1936. *New York Public Library.*

that prioritized balanced budgets and government frugality, the city had cut yearly expenses by $1 million by 1933 and boasted of a balanced annual budget. The South's largest cities contributed about half as much to relief as the average American city, but among the six largest southern cities (Atlanta, Birmingham, Dallas, Houston, Memphis and New Orleans), Dallas spent more on relief in the early years of the Depression than all others except for Birmingham. The city implemented its own version of a WPA-type program in 1931, allowing the unemployed to labor for one day a week on local public works projects. The laborers were paid as little as eighteen cents per hour, but they were paid something. Citizens worked on graveling ten miles of dirt roads, conducting a traffic survey, improving garbage dumps, dredging and cleaning Turtle Creek Lake, building Trinity River levees and constructing additions to the city-county hospital system.[166]

The Civil Works Administration opened a cannery in Dallas, supplying the city with government beef, and vouchers were distributed that could be exchanged for staple foods at grocery stores. In one of the most ambitious relief efforts conducted in the country, the Citizens Emergency Relief Committee oversaw the planting of four hundred acres of Trinity River bottomlands with corn, squash, sweet potatoes, okra and other vegetables. The vegetables were canned and saved for winter or distributed at one of six dining halls the committee ran. The city's utilization of micro-agriculture earned it the distinction of having more gardens producing food for the relief effort than any other southern city.[167]

Particularly hard hit by the Depression was the "Forgotten Man," the white-collar worker who still owned the accoutrements of respectability— the dress clothes of the office worker. The Forgotten Man had neither work nor money, but he did still have his pride, something that kept him from seeking relief, as other unemployed might. If Brooks Coffman had continued working as a salesman, as he had first done when moving to Dallas, he might have counted himself among the Forgotten Men. But he had moved into a federal job, and so could ride out the early years of the Depression with a steady income and a guarantee of employment. His mistress, young Corinne Maddox, likewise enjoyed the stability of federal work. The two could count themselves among the lucky citizens of Dallas.

Lucky in terms of employment, but unlucky in other ways. While other Dallasites struggled with questions of basic survival, Brooks and Corinne deepened their affair. The tree of their union had sprouted a vibrant green, but it would soon begin to show signs of rot. The rot would prove to be deadly, and not only for their relationship.

A Dallas family who left the city for a better life in California. "There's no chance for a fellow to get a holt hisself in this country," the father told the photographer, Dorothea Lange. *New York Public Library.*

IT WAS AN UNROMANTIC spot to visit for sex, but it was private. The gravel pit was abandoned, and the grown-up willows and brush around the Trinity River nearby provided cover from prying eyes. A hundred years before, land speculators had hidden out from Indians in the same thickets. The gravel pit was private, but at least one person had noticed Brooks and Corinne's frequent visits. A deputy sheriff had seen them traveling to the pit several times and had followed them and learned their identities. He had made note of their visits but decided not to confront the couple. "A man's life is his own to live," the officer thought.[168]

A 1938 photo from a pit near Lincoln, Nebraska, gives an idea of what the spot might have looked like when Corinne and Brooks visited. In the photo, a tall, sloping structure of rough-cut wood shields one side of the pit. Piles of gravel rest against a timber retaining wall. The other side of the wall meets the earth at a ninety-degree angle, the piles of gravel shading the corner where the two planes meet.

Corinne Maddox must have felt some disappointment when Brooks brought her to the pit. The other spot they liked to visit was a motel in Dallas. At least there the couple could conduct their relationship with a veneer of legitimacy. At least there the two could lie on a bed with the privacy of walls and a roof. But the motel was expensive.

An account of the couple's affair published a few years later suggested that the deputy sheriff who had followed the couple was not the only person aware of the relationship. Brooks Coffman was a "known ladies' man," one report would say. Corinne's mother and sister, with whom she lived, knew about the affair and tried to convince her that carrying on was a bad idea. Corinne remained "blissfully happy," reassuring them that Brooks would divorce his wife one day. She would later state publicly that she didn't know he was married for two years after beginning the affair. She was holding out hope that the veneer of legitimacy she sometimes felt in the motel would become actual legitimacy—that she would one day become Mrs. Coffman.[169]

Brooks Coffman carried on the affair, providing his mistress with just enough hope to remain in the relationship. But within a few years, his behavior had clued Corinne in to his true intentions. She began to grow skeptical. In 1935, Brooks's wife got pregnant. Corinne told him she didn't mind if he slept with his wife. But Brooks was also seeing other women—Corinne wasn't *the* other woman, but one of a few. The couple began to fight.

The rot had begun, and their relationship had reached a crossroads—it was clearly time to part ways, but neither party would commit to a break. Instead, they took turns shunning each other. When Corinne threatened to leave Brooks, he would pursue her; when she pursued him, he turned away.

The two had become poor horsemen—an analogy used by a reporter who covered their affair years later. Each had been thrown from the saddle. But rather than detach, each had allowed himself or herself to be dragged by the stirrup.

Eventually, Brooks Coffman would prove to be more attached to the affair than Corinne. She made up her mind to leave him sometime in 1936 or 1937 and let him know. He couldn't accept the insult and began "haunting" her—a euphemistic word that might be replaced today with

A Dallas cotton mill worker took material from his factory to make his family a tent before losing his job. Photo by Russell Lee, 1939. *New York Public Library.*

"stalking" or "harassing." His pleading turned to threats, and in 1938, Corinne was disturbed enough that she sought legal action against her former lover. She asked a local justice of the peace to force Brooks to sign a "peace bond," a legal agreement to cease the harassment or face legal consequences.

The peace bond seemed to give Corinne some relief for a time. But by 1939, the harassment had started up again. Corinne would go to work and notice Coffman hanging around her building. The situation came to a head on May 20, 1939.

Brooks asked Corinne to go to a soda fountain with him. He had a proposition for her—a permanent fix for the conundrum the two had found themselves in for the past six years. "I'm going to California," Brooks told Corinne over drinks. "I wish you'd go with me."

It was the commitment Corinne had been craving years before—Brooks would leave his wife, devote all his attention to Corinne and start fresh. But by the time Brooks finally offered to put Corinne first, it was far too late. Corinne, truly over the man, laughed in his face. "Not this time," she said.

Brooks Coffman stifled his rage, feigning indifference. He told her that he still wanted to be friends. He offered to drive her home. He had to get her in his car one last time.

She bought the ruse and slid into his passenger seat. But he did not drive the young blonde home. Instead, he headed for the spot where they had spent so many private moments—the abandoned gravel pit. He had asked Corinne to flee to California. Now he would coerce her. He parked at the gravel pit and began insisting that Corinne leave with him. She maintained her refusal. It was too much for Brooks to bear.

He opened the driver's side door and stepped out, his fist closing on an ice pick he had brought along. He walked around to the passenger's side door, yanked it open and brought the pick down on Corinne. It sank into the flesh of her back. She screamed and twisted away. Brooks stabbed twice more, this time piercing her chest. Raising her hands in defense, Corinne felt one of her fingers snap. Brooks was cursing her all along. If you won't be with me, he told her, you won't be with anyone.

He grabbed Corinne by the throat and pulled her from the car, slamming her into the mud of the pit. He began squeezing, cutting off her air. It was clear he intended to murder her, and it looked like he would succeed. But something inside her—perhaps voluntary, perhaps not—told her to go limp. Go limp. Go limp. He might let go. It worked. Brooks released his grip on her throat and let her seemingly lifeless body fall back into a puddle. "That finishes you," he said, giving her one last look before climbing into his car and driving away.

But Corinne was not dead. She mustered the strength to crawl out of the pit and to a road nearby. She had lost her skirt and shoes sometime during the struggle. She was covered in mud and could do little more than lie by the side of the road. But a driver spotted her and took her to the hospital. The police met her there, and she told them what had happened. Brooks Coffman had tried to murder her. Soon there was a warrant out for his arrest. He would be tried for assault with intent to murder.

## POOR HORSEMEN, PART III: CORINNE'S REVENGE

Brooks did not try to flee. Perhaps realizing that he'd never be able to escape, perhaps feeling genuinely remorseful, he turned himself in. But he didn't stay in jail—a judge set a $5,000 bond, and soon Brooks was out.[170]

As Corinne recovered in the hospital, Brooks thought about the trial that would take place in six months. And he thought about Corinne. He had tried to kill her, but he still cared for her. He thought he should send a card to the hospital, something to let her know he was sorry and that he was praying for her. He found one:

*From one who is praying for your recovery—*
*My heartfelt wish for you today*
*Is put within a prayer*
*That he who watches over all*
*In tender love and care*
*May ease the hour of your distress*
*Your health and strength renew*
*And speed the day which brings you back*
*To those who pray for you.*

It was perfect. He sent it off.

After reading the words, Corinne tucked the card under her pillow. She recovered at the hospital for several weeks until she felt well enough to go home. Her broken finger leaving her unable to type, she lost her job as a stenographer.

Corinne would ride the Dallas streetcar in the months before the trial and sometimes find Brooks Coffman waiting for her at her stop. The man just could not leave his former lover alone. Brooks would ask Corinne if she'd like to have a cup of coffee. She would refuse, and twice his temper flared. Twice he slapped her so hard she fell to the ground.

As Brooks's trial moved closer, Corinne steeled herself for what she would have to say in court. But it wasn't like going on record about the affair, and about Brooks's abuse, was anything new. She had told police everything shortly after the attack. She had told the justice of the peace about the threats.

One day in the months leading up the trial, the phone rang at Corinne's house. It was Brooks. He had another message for her. This time he wasn't calling to let her know he was praying for her or to ask her out to coffee— instead, he warned her. Don't testify, he told her. If you do, I'll kill you. Corinne weighed the threat and in the end decided she would not testify. When Brooks's trial date came on October 9, Corinne didn't show. Brooks's trial was postponed indefinitely.

The six months of terror Corinne had endured since her stabbing at the gravel pit had led her to a conclusion: she no longer had faith that the justice system was the answer or that it could protect her. She would speed up the judicial process, make sure that Brooks could never hurt her again. She acquired the means of making it so and decided that she would not be stalked by Brooks any longer. Instead, she would become the stalker. And at the right moment, she would end Brooks Coffman's life.[171]

It took Corinne Maddox three weeks to find her opportunity. She had acquired an old top-break .38-caliber revolver. The gun, sometimes called a "Tramp's Terror," was cheap, accurate and easy to conceal and use. It was favored as a backup or "just in case" weapon. But the gun was not a "man-stopper," as one writer put it. Corinne began hanging around the city blocks where she might catch Brooks walking, her compact revolver loaded and ready. Her plan was to shoot him down in the street and then surrender.[172]

On November 1, she spotted Brooks walking and decided the time was right. She took aim and pulled the trigger of her .38, and the internal hammer of the gun first cocked and then clicked. But the powder inside the cartridge did not fire. Brooks, all the while, walked on, unaware that he had just avoided his own assassination.

Corinne, spooked, turned and fled, but not before a friend of hers saw her. The friend had seen the gun in Corinne's hand and had seen the failed murder, but for some reason she did not report Corinne.

Three more weeks passed, and Corinne spent the time planning. She took her revolver to a gunsmith and had it serviced. She bought a shoulder holster for the gun. She acquired a second pistol—this time a .32-caliber pocket automatic. The pistol was practically designed for Corinne's purpose. Sleek and compact, the pistol fit into her handbag easily and wouldn't snag when she was ready to pull it out. The pistol was a favorite of Bonnie Parker—and of Frank Hamer, the federal agent who eventually took her down. It shot "rather anemic little rounds," one writer put it, "but they still hurt at close range, which was no doubt the intended purpose."[173]

Corinne now had two guns—neither particularly powerful but deadly at close range. She filled her guns with lead bullets, hoping that they'd find their mark but not ricochet and hit anyone else. She decided that she'd kill him at his favorite restaurant this time. She arrived and took a table. She waited, but he didn't show.

Again, she resolved to catch him on the street. She awoke at 7:00 a.m. on November 20 and began getting dressed. She put on a stylish black suit that fastened with two jeweled clips and a lacy, black cossack hat. Her fingernails were long and manicured. She decided that she would visit a beauty shop along a route she knew Brooks took to work. And

An ad for one of the pistols Corinne Maddox used to kill Brooks Coffman, from the 1916 Montgomery Ward Company catalogue. *Internet Archive.*

then, at around 8:45 a.m., she spotted him. He was walking on Main Street, and he was walking with another other woman—Flora Allen, a different pretty young stenographer he'd met at the office. Allen was a year younger than Corinne.

This time, she would not fail. Grabbing the revolver from its holster and the automatic from her handbag, Corinne ran up behind Brooks and began pulling triggers. This time, the guns cracked. Brooks fell to the ground. Flora ran. Onlookers gasped. Then, as one account described:

*He staggered to his feet, lurched across the street, like a wounded animal seeking shelter from the huntress. Corinne was not to be daunted. She followed him, still shooting.*

*The guns cracked 11 times. Two bullets struck, and one passed through Brook's left lung—the fatal shot. Brooks fell again. He tried pushing himself up, but no longer had the strength. He used the last of his breath to beg Corinne for mercy. But it was too late. He lasted another two hours.*[174]

Corinne, her job finished, strode away from the bloody scene. She took an envelope from her purse and handed it to a passerby. "You give him that," she said. She then walked into a telegraph office and placed her two guns on the office counter. She'd like to call the sheriff's office, she said. She'd like to surrender.

Police picked her up, and she told them everything. Her bond was set at $7,500, and by the end of the day she was back home with her mother and sister. "I'll get a good night's sleep tonight, for the first time in six months," she told a reporter as she left the courthouse. "I feel better right now than I have for a long time."[175]

The next day, Corinne sat before a grand jury of twelve Dallas men and explained the torment she had endured over the past six months. The details of her story were never released to the press, but after hearing her tell her story for more than an hour, District Attorney Andrew Patton told reporters, "There's a lot more to this case that hasn't been told yet."[176]

It didn't take the grand jury long to decide whether to prosecute Corinne for murder. The same day, they wrote two words across her bill of indictment: no bill. Corinne would not be prosecuted for murder and was free to go.

Brooks Coffman never got to read the note Corinne wrote for him and handed to a passerby on the day he died. But the contents of the note made their way into the press:

*To you*
*Who caused me all my pain and grief*
*And later prayed for my recovery*
*Why? So if I lived you could torture me?*
*It couldn't have been for my relief*
*Because upon my life you've made more threats*
*As in your prayer*
*I lived and came back to thee*

*But back for back*
*And now I'm forced to do this*
*It is with deep regret*
*May God have mercy on us both*

*CORINNE*[177]

## Part IV

# THE CLASH OF WILLS IN MIDCENTURY DALLAS

## THE COWBOY WHO KILLED A CAT, PART I: COLLATERAL DAMAGE

Eighteen thousand people showed up for Benny Binion's eighty-third birthday in Las Vegas. Celebrities like Gene Autry, Willie Nelson and Hank Williams Jr. were there. So were scores of representatives of the underworld. The eighteen thousand well-wishers had come to honor the aging and beloved patriarch. A net worth of $100 million meant a lot of friends. It also meant a fair share of enemies. But one enemy, perhaps the most important one, was not at the celebration. He had been taken care of decades ago. Finally. After thirteen attempts.

IN 1926, TWENTY-TWO-YEAR-OLD BENNY Binion broke with his mentor and boss, Warren Diamond. Binion set up his own gambling operation at the Southland Hotel. It was a bold, dangerous move—exactly the kind of gamble that made Binion a legend. For some reason, Diamond never challenged his rebellious protégé, and when he committed suicide seven years later, Binion became the most powerful gambler in Dallas. And the most dangerous.

Although he was known as a generous employer and frequently rewarded his strongmen and runners with unexpected gifts, it was widely known that you did not cross Benny Binion. One runner learned the hard way when

Benny Binion. *Josh Foreman.*

Binion stabbed a pencil through his eye for trying to pocket some of his boss's money. A number of other runners were found along the Trinity River, their bodies riddled with bullets. Binion was only charged with two murders (one homicide was given a suspended sentence, and he beat the other by claiming self-defense), but Dallasites knew that the law at the time all too often took an accommodating attitude toward vice—as long as fines and tributes came on time.

Binion's business boomed over the next two decades. But at the end of World War II, reform candidates stormed into office, and Binion could read the writing on the wall. He packed his bags and moved to Las Vegas, which at the time had only two casinos. He continued, however, to oversee his illicit Dallas trade. The tributes continued to pour in. That is, most of the tributes. One man, Herbert Noble, refused to acknowledge his "Cowboy Boss." A Dallas police captain reported, "It was the first time someone had actually defied him and lived. He was losing face with everybody in the rackets."[178] Benny Binion wasn't the kind of man to lose face.

*Assassination Attempt no. 1*
*January 12, 1946*

Herbert Noble locked up the Dallas Airmen's Club and walked to his Mercury coupe. As he unlocked the doors, he noticed a Cadillac parked down the street. Noble got in his vehicle and pulled away. The Cadillac followed. Noble began making erratic and random turns to see if the Cadillac would follow. It did.

Noble raced up and down the city streets. He was determined to lead his pursuers away from his family home in Oak Cliff and hit the highway for his ranch in Denton. Once on the highway, the Cadillac quickly caught up. A mile from his ranch, the Cadillac pulled up alongside him. A man leaned out the passenger back seat and fired a sawed-off shotgun at Noble. He was immediately covered in bits of glass. A second shotgun blast rang in his ears and then several .45 pistol shots. Still,

Noble remained unscathed. He began to return fire, one hand on the wheel and one wielding his gun.

Not surprisingly, he soon ran his car off the road and into a ditch. He scrambled out, leaving his gun behind, and ran toward a farmhouse. Two of his assassins jumped out of the Cadillac and began firing at their fleeing victim. One of the bullets hit Noble in the lower back just as he reached the house. Noble hit the ground and crawled under the raised house. Fortunately, a pack of dogs were roused by the noise, and a neighbor turned on his floodlights and stepped onto his porch armed with a .30-30. This was, after all, Texas. Noble's would-be assassins fled to the Cadillac and drove off in a cloud of dust.[179]

Herbert Noble. *Josh Foreman.*

Believing himself to be mortally wounded, Noble asked his neighbor to hold a flashlight while he wrote a farewell note to his wife, Mildred.[180] But Herbert Noble survived the assassination attempt. He would survive the next eleven attempts as well. Ironically, it would be Mildred who first succumbed to an assassin's plot.

HERBERT NOBLE WAS A West Dallas tough. He grew up just a few blocks from the Barrow and Parker families on the wrong side of town, and like nearly everyone in West Dallas, he longed to get out. Against the odds, Noble made it through school until he was sixteen. He got a respectable job at a refinery and then a trucking company. He married a beautiful woman named Mildred. He fathered a healthy daughter. And then he stole a car, was given a two-year suspended sentence and disappeared from the records for six years.

When Noble returned to Dallas in 1938, he had enough money to rent a house in Oak Cliff, possessed a pilot's license and had a penchant for gambling. He quickly found himself employed as a "manager" at the Santa Paula Hotel in downtown Dallas. In reality, he managed the illegal casino of boss Sam Murray and served as Murray's bodyguard and muscle.

But then, in 1938, Murray was assassinated in front of the Dallas National Bank by Benny Binion's henchman Ivy Miller. Noble quickly took control of

A panorama of Dallas, circa 1910. *Library of Congress.*

his former boss's operations. When he began to pay Binion the customary tribute, the Dallas underworld put one and one together. Noble had been absent when Sam Murray drove to Dallas National Bank. He was also the only one who knew where his boss would be traveling—alone. One phone call and a few months later, Herbert Noble was one of the most powerful gambling bosses in Dallas.

*Assassination Attempt no. 2*
*August 19, 1946*

Herbert Noble received a call from his associate, Jack Darby, who ran several crap games with Noble. Darby told his partner that he had collected $12,000 in cash, half of which was Noble's. Darby claimed that he had been drinking and wanted some backup transporting the cash. Noble agreed to meet him at the Biltmore Recreation Room.

When he arrived, Darby pulled a .38 pistol and ordered the shocked Noble upstairs, where two other Dallas gamblers awaited him. As he walked up the stairs, Darby fired two shots into the floor by Noble's feet. Inside the room, he jeered and taunted and cursed Noble, all the while threatening him with his pistol. The other two gamblers observed the scene. They were to be witnesses when Noble finally had enough and drew his own gun. Darby would then shoot him in self-defense. Noble never took the bait. His restraint saved his life.

In the end, Darby decided not to kill him, and Noble walked away and returned to his wife and child.[181]

Benny Binion was determined to be the godfather of Dallas gambling. (He soon would be.) He was going to control the entire racket. He didn't

mind if other would-be bosses wanted a piece of the action, but they were going to have to pay him. Most did. But one didn't.

Herbert Noble had been an associate of Binion's, but then he decided to strike out on his own. This was not an unusual move, and the transition should have been smooth—as long as he paid Binion the customary 25 percent of profits. Besides, Binion actually liked Noble. Even more so with rival Sam Murray out of the picture.

At first, the two gamblers—the overlord and the protégé—coexisted. Both became wealthy. Noble's Airmen's Club was a huge success, and he made sure that Binion got his take.

But then Binion upped the payoff to 40 percent of the profits. Noble decided that his boss had gone too far. There was a big difference between 25 percent and 40 percent. He simply refused to pay. In fact, he told Binion to "go straight to hell."[182]

*Assassination Attempt no. 3*
*May 21, 1948*

Herbert Noble turned off the county road toward his house, slowing down as he drove over the cattle guard. Suddenly, he heard a loud blast. Glass shattered all around him. Almost instantaneously, he felt a pain tear through his right hand, wrist and arm. Double-aught buckshot.

Noble drove as quickly as he could to his house. He stumbled in, coated in blood, and told his wife what had happened. He then drove to a neighbor, who took him to the hospital.

When queried as to the reason for the visit, Noble told the doctor that he was cleaning his pistol and accidentally dropped it on the ground, causing it to go off. When the doctor examined his near-mutilated arm, Noble reluctantly changed his story: he dropped the gun and it went off five consecutive times.[183]

*Assassination Attempt no. 4*
*September 8, 1949*

An unknown black Ford drove slowly up and down the county road outside Noble's ranch in Denton. It had been on the same road the past four days. One of Noble's neighbors came and told him that it was back.

Noble had just dropped his wife and daughter off at his ranch after a family trip to Grapevine. He grabbed his pistol and .30-caliber carbine and recruited one of his ranch hands to ride with him. The two drove to the intersection, turned the car lights out and waited.

They didn't have to wait long. Minutes later, the Ford was back. When it passed them, driving slowly by Noble's house, Noble turned his lights on and began to trail them. The Ford zoomed off with Noble in pursuit. Six miles later, the Ford ran off the highway and into a ditch. Noble jumped out of his own car, carbine in hand. He shouted for the men in the Ford to come out. They did, pistols and shotgun in hand. The three would-be assassins fired on Noble, who promptly returned fire. Noble was shot in the leg just above the ankle, but he continued to shoot at his assailants until all three fled into the woods.

He told reporters, "They'll get me yet. They want me out of the way so they can take over my business." Herbert "The Cat" Noble had survived a fourth assassination attempt.[184]

*Assassination Attempt no. 5*
*November 29, 1949*

Noble turned on the engine in the Mercury sedan. The explosion was heard miles away. Window panes in nearby houses and cars shattered. Thousands of shards imbedded themselves in Noble's body before it was blown ten feet away. The leg below the right knee flew off in a different direction. A neighbor ran outside but had no idea who the mangled corpse was.

The contract on Noble was finally fulfilled.[185] Only it was the wrong Noble.

Herbert Noble had driven his wife's Cadillac to Fort Worth to sign the papers that would make him co-owner of Hicks Field, an airfield where he planned to repair and store private airplanes and eventually build a manufacturing facility. If things went according to plan, Herbert Noble would retire from the gambling racket.

His wife, Mildred, was thrilled. She planned to celebrate that night with a romantic candlelight dinner. She got into Herbert's Mercury to go pick up her maid and turned the key to start the engine.[186]

Three days later, a distraught and broken Herbert Noble joined seven hundred other mourners as they laid his beloved wife's thousand-pound bronze casket—the largest ever built in Dallas—into the ground.[187]

## THE COWBOY WHO KILLED A CAT, PART II: SUCCESS

*Revenge*
*December 24, 1950*

Around one o'clock in the morning, Lois Green, a trusted Binion hitman, stepped out of his headquarters at the Sky Vue Club. He and his fellow gangster associates had spent the night drinking, talking and plotting. He walked to his nearby green Oldsmobile and prepared to get in. Then he heard a sound in the dark alley behind him. He turned around to greet dozens of shotgun pellets. A second blast tore into his neck and side as Green stumbled around to the front of his car. The assassin fired once more and disappeared into the dark alley.

Moments later, with Jack Todd, Green's right-hand man, and a who's who of the Dallas underworld around him, Lois Green died the way he always expected and feared.

A Dallas preacher-convict presided at his funeral and told the gathering of showgirls, pimps, burglars and murderers that "[Green] lived in a world of his own and was loved and respected in it."[188]

The day of the funeral, Herbert Noble walked into his friend's grocery store and exclaimed, "There he is. There's the dirty son of a bitch," as he put a picture of mutilated Lois Green on the counter.[189]

*Assassination Attempt no. 6*
*December 31, 1949*

Noble's daughter, Freda, was about to return to school in Virginia. But first, she had a date in Dallas. Herbert, with his wife now deceased five weeks, wanted to spend the evening with Freda, and so he asked her to invite the boyfriend over to his place. Noble invited one of his friends as well.

Before the guests arrived, Noble decided to make a run to the drugstore. He walked out the front door and was immediately lit up by a huge spotlight. A second later, a rifle bullet tore through his left elbow, shattered his hip and lodged in his spine. He stumbled backward as a second bullet sped past him, hitting the brick wall next to the door he was pounding on. Freda opened it, and Noble collapsed on the floor inside. Shortly after, he was taken to Methodist hospital, where he told police officers that two men had yet again tried to kill him. Yet again they failed.

Benny Binion was beginning to lose patience. So was Herbert Noble. He told reporters from his hospital bed, "I am afraid I am going to have to take the law into my own hands. I can't go on any longer like this. I am at the end of the road. I have held off because of my daughter Freida [*sic*] and because I have tried to live right. I am a gambler and have been, that is true, but I have never done anything to deserve these attacks, not only on myself and my dead wife, but the danger it might bring to others." He went on to say the most recent attack was by far the most painful—"except the suffering I had when they blew up my wife."[190]

Within days, Noble had his brother wire some money to a friend of Ralph Capone—the brother of Al Capone—as a down payment on Binion's life.

The evening of his surgery, police had found in Noble's pocket a detailed map and photograph of Binion's ranch in Las Vegas.[191]

*Assassination Attempt no. 7*
*February 6, 1950*

He had been in Methodist Hospital for six weeks. He was beginning to feel better, although his arm still hurt. Around eleven o'clock at night, with a full bladder, Noble turned on the bedside lamp and pushed himself out of bed. He had taken only a few steps toward the bathroom when a .30-caliber carbine bullet smashed through the window and whizzed by the top of his head. Instinctively—and now used to bullets flying around him—Noble hit the floor. A friend who had been staying with him ran down the hall and into the room, where he crawled to the lamp and unplugged it.

Noble told reporters, "I know if I go out of here that I will be killed. I just don't know what to do." As if to confirm his suspicions, Methodist Hospital began to get hundreds of inquiries asking when exactly Herbert Noble would be released.[192]

*April 12, 1950*

Herbert Noble was not going to let the latest attempt on his life slide. He, too, knew how to kill. And he was determined to make Benny Binion understand this.

Noble thoroughly enjoyed flying. He once told a friend that he only ever felt truly safe when he was in the air. He flew his plane to inspect his ranch. He flew it for pleasure. He flew it to and from Mexico, many times. So many times, in fact, that the law began to suspect that Noble was engaged in some sort of illicit traffic south of the border, either stolen goods or drugs.

On this particular day, he planned to fly for an entirely different reason. He was going to send Benny Binion to a fiery death. Binion had come at him with guns and dynamite. Noble would retaliate with two military surplus bombs, one high explosive and the other incendiary.

Binion had been orchestrating the assassination attempts from his home in Las Vegas. Worried about being arrested on an old gambling charge

*The Card Players*, by Paul Cézanne, 1890–92. *Metropolitan Museum of Art.*

should he set foot in Texas, Binion had settled in much more lenient Nevada. He, his wife and their five children lived in a residential neighborhood. The family (and neighbors) would have to be collateral damage.

Noble was in the process of attaching two bomb racks underneath the wings of his plane when police lieutenant George Butler came to see if he had any useful information regarding the Dallas underworld. Normally, the two, lawman and career criminal, had a working relationship. On this day, however, Noble whipped out his carbine and aimed it at Butler.

"What the hell are you doing, Herbert? Put that rifle down."

Noble hesitated and then lowered his carbine and dropped to his knees in tears. He was tired of the assassination attempts. Tired of the sleepless nights. Tired of battling a man who seemingly got all the breaks. Tired of his wife's murderers being still on the loose. Tired of Benny Binion.

Noble admitted to his plot to bomb the Binion residence. He handed over a detailed map and promised Lieutenant Butler not to drop any bombs from his plane.[193]

*Assassination Attempt no. 8*
*June 13, 1950*

Franklin Strong and Leroy Gloss set up their deer blind. They expected their prey to use this particular access point, and when it did…well, they were armed with twelve-gauge shotguns.

Herbert Noble awoke from his usual sleeping pill–induced rest of several hours. It had been his routine lately to pace his ranch house all night long, periodically peeking out the blinds for intruders and would-be assassins. He kept six Chihuahua dogs inside the house—"They're not worth a damn as guard dogs, but they sure raise hell if they hear anything." He had also taken to drinking copious amounts of alcohol and taking pills to stay awake until it was time for his sleeping pill, as well as midnight drives into West Dallas in the drunken hopes of finding his wife's murderers.

At 9:00 a.m., Herbert Noble steered his car onto the road that would take him to Dallas. A blast from a twelve-gauge shotgun blew out one front tire. More shots smashed into his car. "I had left the ranch and was about a half mile down the road when I heard bullets whipping about the car. Heavy timber lined the road and I couldn't see anyone." He put his foot to the accelerator and, one mile later, pulled into a neighbor's driveway, calmly called the police and proceeded to change his tire.[194]

*Assassination Attempt no. 9*
*November 19, 1950*

Herbert Noble saw the blaze from his house window. Six or seven assassination attempts earlier, he might have stormed out, guns blazing to punish the arsonists. But now, with a body riddled with bullets, he knew better. The burning barn wasn't the target of the night's attack; it was the bait. Noble remained inside his home until the fire department arrived.[195]

*January 23, 1951*

Herbert Noble noticed Binion associate Jack Todd's black Oldsmobile parked outside Sonny's Food Store. Todd was out on bond and awaiting a trial for transporting jellied nitroglycerine. Noble parked his own car and waited for Todd to exit the store. When he did, Noble ordered him into his car. "Get in the car, Jack, or I'll shoot your damn brains out." With one hand on a .30 rifle and the other on the wheel, Noble drove his captive—with the headlights off—toward Fort Worth. Unable to cover Todd and drive at the same time, Noble ran his car into a ditch. The two began furiously fighting over the rifle.

When two nearby police officers finally got to the car, they came upon a free-for-all with both men desperately hanging on to the same gun. The two were eventually separated and disarmed. Todd was sent on his way, while Noble was taken to Methodist Hospital to receive fifty-six stitches to repair his ear that had been nearly bitten off in the melee. After being booked and bailed out, he was set free as well.

Noble claimed, "I only wanted to find out where he got that jellied dynamite. It was exactly the same kind I found under my car in downtown Dallas two years ago this Valentine's day. It was exactly the same kind used to murder my wife." He later told reporters, "I'm not ashamed of anything I've done. It doesn't look like the law is doing anything about my wife's murder. But I'll never forget it."[196]

*Assassination Attempt no. 10*
*February 13, 1951*

At 2:20 a.m., a large bundle of dynamite sticks was hurled toward the front glass door of Noble's Dallas Airmen's Club. A tremendous explosion destroyed much of the club, but otherwise there were no injuries in the empty club. Perhaps the assassins had misinformation on Noble's whereabouts, or perhaps it was a warning that Noble would meet the same fate as his wife sooner or later.[197]

*Assassination Attempt no. 11*
*March 22, 1951*

Noble had a massive ranch to patrol. He used to do it from his jeep, but the increasingly frequent attempts on his life—as well as the death of his wife via car bomb—convinced him to make the rounds by plane. It didn't matter—Benny Binion was going to kill him one way or another.

Noble turned on the engine of his plane; it exploded. Fortunately, the steel firewall protected Noble himself. He climbed out without a scratch.

"I got into my plane about 6 p.m., planning to do some practice flying and look over the cattle in the pastures. When I turned on the engine the

Herbert Noble spent much of his time outside Dallas at a ranch in Denton County, Texas. *Denton Public Library/Wikimedia Commons.*

prop moved about four inches and blew up in my face."[198] When the police arrived, they found parts of the plane more than one hundred feet away and nitroglycerin gel in the generator—the same substance that had caused his wife's fiery death.[199]

*Assassination Attempt no. 12*
*March 28, 1951*

Noble tried to ignite the engine in his recently repaired plane. Nothing happened. He tried again. Same result. He climbed down to inspect the engine and found nitroglycerin gel in two of his engine cylinders. Noble knew who was behind these assassination attempts, yet he didn't know who the demolition "expert" was who kept trying to bomb him. But whoever he was, he sure was persistent.[200]

*Assassination Attempt no. 13: Success*
*August 7, 1951*

For Herbert Noble, the number thirteen indeed proved unlucky. He drove his 1950 Ford sedan from his ranch house, Diamond M Ranch, to his mailbox. He lowered his window and reached to get his mail. He would never get a chance to read it.

An hour and a half later, Noble's neighbor drove to his own mailbox and found a grisly sight. Noble's mailbox had been replaced by a four-by-five-foot crater. The hood of Noble's car lay forty feet away, and the rest was flipped upside down next to the crater.

Herbert Noble himself was scattered ten yards in each direction, with pieces hanging over a nearby barbed wire fence. He was identified by his head, shoulders and arms. One of his legs lay thirty yards away in the middle of the road. The rest of him lay scattered in the noonday Texas sun.

Inside his car, investigators found a .30-caliber carbine. Next to the demolished car of the man who dared cross gambling boss Benny Binion lay two playing cards: an ace of diamonds and a joker.[201]

BENNY BINION WOULD GO on to serve a three-and-a-half-year prison sentence at Leavenworth for tax evasion. Upon his release in October 1957, he returned to Las Vegas, where he would spend the last half of his life, quickly

Benny Binion bought property on Fremont Street in Las Vegas the same year Herbert Noble died. The casino he built there soon became a staple of Las Vegas gambling. *Library of Congress.*

becoming one of the most successful and wealthy casino operators, as well as the father of the World Series of Poker.

Because Benny couldn't hold a gambling license, his wife, Teddy Jane, and son, Jack, ran his Horseshoe casino, leaving Benny to hold court each day at a corner booth, regaling his admirers with stories from the Dallas gambling war of the '40s and '50s.[202]

## AVENGING DALLAS'S STAIN

*November 22, 1963*
*12:30 p.m.*
*Dallas, Texas*

Jacob Rubenstein was bantering with acquaintances at the office of the *Dallas Morning News.* He could often be found in these crowded, hectic

President John F. Kennedy's official portrait, painted posthumously by Aaron Shikler. *The White House Historical Association/Wikimedia Commons.*

offices. The atmosphere suited him very much—people on the move, hustle and bustle, important events and gossip disseminating. Jacob knew that he was important and enjoyed being in the midst of important happenings.

And then there was his business. He ran two clubs in Dallas, and he relied on the paper for advertising. Sometimes he paid his bill on time, sometimes he arrived with the previous week's late payment. Today, he brought both. He had a special show planned for Saturday and Sunday.

Suddenly, all was chaos in the building. There had been a shooting five blocks away. Another day in Dallas, another murder (107 people would be murdered in Dallas in 1963).[203] But this murder was different. Jacob knew the man who had been killed. The victim was important to him. So was the victim's wife. And his now orphaned children. Jacob was beside himself. Normally loquacious, he stood in stunned silence. Then he crowded into a manager's office and watched the horrifying bulletins scroll across the television. Still stunned, he walked to a reporter's desk and phoned his sister, Eva.

Eva was crying. Jacob listened to her grief and then passed the phone to the reporter. "[You] want other people to feel that you feel emotionally disturbed the same way as other people, so I let John listen to the phone that my sister was crying hysterically."[204]

Jacob then left the paper's offices after canceling the advertisements. Out of respect, he would close his two clubs for the weekend.[205]

*Childhood, 1920s*
*Chicago, Illinois*

Jacob Rubenstein had far from an idyllic childhood. He was the son of an alcoholic, abusive father who was frequently arrested for beating his wife and a neurotic mother who resented her eight pregnancies. Rejected at home, Jacob turned to the streets. At eleven years old, he was referred by Jewish social workers to the Institute for Juvenile Research, where a psychiatric report determined that young Jacob was "quick tempered" and "disobedient." "He is egocentric and expects much attention, but is unable to get it as there are many children at home." Jacob would spend the rest of his adolescence bouncing between foster homes and living with his clinically psychotic mother.

Despite Jacob's rarely attending school (by choice), both Rubenstein parents insisted that Jacob learn at least the basics of their Orthodox Jewish faith. When his father was around, Jacob accompanied him to synagogue.

He observed the Jewish dietary practices and feast days. He even learned a little Hebrew. His parents might be dysfunctional, but they wanted their children raised in the faith of their ancestors.

Jacob would be beaten as a child, bullied when he did attend school and experience his own mental collapse. His life would descend into chaos. But he would never forget his Jewish roots. He would fight for the honor of that heritage. And time proved that he was prepared to kill for it as well.[206]

*November 22, 1963*
*1:33 p.m.*
*Dallas, Texas*

Jacob Rubenstein heard via television that the wounded man had been taken to Parkland Hospital and was in critical condition. Always a man to appear at any "spectacle," Jacob showed up at the hospital. Shortly after, he received the chilling news that the patient was no more. The bullet that had shattered his head had caused his death.

Jacob was devastated. "I felt like a nothing person, like the world had ended—I did not want to go on living anymore."[207] He sullenly drove to his club and promptly began contacting his workers and telling them not to bother coming in that weekend. "I felt like a nothing person. My first thought was to close the club. I was afraid I would crack up. Such a great person, and then to be snuffed out." He called his sister Eva again, as well as another sister, Eileen, in Chicago. He told this latter sister that he was going to fly to Chicago, that he needed to get away, that he was on the verge of a breakdown. Instead, Eileen convinced him to remain in Dallas and look after the distraught Eva. Jacob agreed and then called his doctor and asked when the synagogue service would be held that night.

Jacob planned to spend the evening in prayer for the man he had cared so deeply about.[208]

Jack Ruby after his arrest on November 24, 1963. *National Archives.*

*Early Adulthood, 1930s*
*Chicago, Illinois*

Jacob Rubenstein wanted to be accepted, to be liked. But he was a Jew in the 1930s. No matter what he did or how he behaved, there would be many who disliked and even hated him. He resolved, nevertheless, to make a success of himself and to never forget he was a Jew.

Jacob walked into the Rubenstein house with blood on his shirt and busted knuckles. To his younger brother, Earl, it was a common sight. Some punk in the streets of Chicago had made an anti-Semitic remark, and Jacob had made him pay for it. Evidently, this time, Jacob had used his fists, although Earl knew that anything lying around that could be used as a club was always a possibility. Earl remembered the day when his elder brother returned home with his clothes splattered in copious amounts of blood belonging to another anti-Semite.

A NUMBER OF PRO-HITLER German Americans were having a rally.
"Heil, Hitler!"
"The trade unions are a Moscow-controlled, Jew conspiracy!"
"To hell with Franklin D. Rosenfeld and the Jew Deal!"
"The Jews are anti-American Bolsheviks!"
The American Nazi rhetoric ceased when Jacob and his fellow "inferiors" disrupted the meeting. That evening, Jacob had another suit to wash and knuckles to ice.

AT THIRTY-TWO, JACOB WAS offered the opportunity—or, rather, was required—to fight the enemies of his nation and his race: Nazi Germany. In 1943, Jacob was drafted into the U.S. Air Force, where he helped the war effort by servicing airplanes as a mechanic. He left the service with an honorable discharge despite beating up a sergeant who had called him a "Jew bastard."[209]

*1947*
*Dallas, Texas*

Jacob received word from Dallas that his sister Eva had been arrested. Apparently, she and her lover, Dr. Waldon Duncan, had been arrested on a fraud charge. Jacob traveled to Dallas to bail his sister out. He decided to stay and help her run her recently opened restaurant, Singapore Supper Club. However, Eva and Jacob fought constantly. "She was temperamental and belligerent. I have been close to her, not that I wanted to be, and wherever I went I couldn't shake her." Jacob gave his sister $300 and asked her to leave. As soon as she moved to California, Jacob changed the restaurant's name to the Silver Spur.

The man formerly known as the "Chicago Cowboy" was in Dallas to stay. He soon after would begin to use another name altogether.[210]

*August 29, 1963*
*Dallas, Texas*

Eva Rubenstein remained in California a few years. Eventually, she and Jacob patched up their differences, and she returned to Dallas.

Now, after a hot summer day near the end of August, Jacob and Eva were on their way to dinner. They were taking their sister Eileen, who was visiting from Chicago, out to dinner. Jacob drove as he normally did, recklessly, in and out of traffic. (He had received tickets for twenty major traffic violations since his arrival in Dallas, and he had had his license suspended for a year in 1959.) His driving became even more erratic when he turned to slap Eva across the face. The two continued to scream at each other, and Jacob slammed on his brakes and threw his sister out of the car. He sped off, leaving her stranded.[211]

*November 22, 1963*
*3:15 p.m.*
*Dallas, Texas*

Jacob sought comfort with his now-reconciled sister Eva. Both had been devastated by the events of the past few hours. He stopped at the Ritz Delicatessen and bought six bottles of celery tonic, a pound of smoked salmon, a pound of roast beef, a pound of smoked white fish, a pound of tongue, bread, onions, oranges and six cakes. It was an incredible amount of food for just two people, but Jacob was depressed. "I figured I'd get drunk on it, it will kill you." Brother and sister gorged themselves on food, watched television and wept for the slain.

Soon, a news report came out that the murderer had been captured. He was a former U.S. marine who had recently returned stateside after defecting

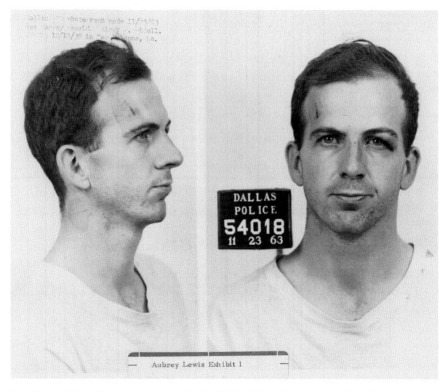

Lee Harvey Oswald's mugshot, taken by the Dallas Police Department after his arrest on November 23, 1963. *National Archives.*

to the Soviet Union. Eva was incensed and exclaimed, "That lousy commie. Don't worry. The commie. We'll get him."

Usually talkative and certainly quick-tempered, Jacob sat silently. After a moment, he stood up, walked to the bathroom and proceeded to throw up.[212]

*1951–62*
*Dallas, Texas*

"Kike Jew!" Jacob whipped around and slugged the offending mouth. The man went home that night with a missing tooth.

*1951*

Willis Dickerson was a guitarist employed by Jacob in one of his clubs. It wasn't a bad gig. Once Jacob's employees got used to his quick temper and accepted the fact that they would be chewed out and "fired" numerous times if they stayed working for him, and that sometimes their paychecks would be a few days late, they didn't mind him. Besides, Willis got to play music and was paid for it.

That all changed the day he told his boss to "go to hell." Jacob immediately threw his employee to the ground, picked him up, pinned him to the wall and kicked him in the groin. Willis retaliated by biting Jacob's left index finger so badly that it had to be amputated.

### *1958*

A foolish patron drew a gun and threatened Jacob Rubenstein. Jacob wrestled the gun from him and proceeded to beat the man to the point of death. He then calmly put the pistol back in the unconscious man's pocket, lifted him up and threw him down the stairs.

Later that year, Jacob arrived at Congregation Shearith Israel to say prayers for his recently deceased father. Noticing the cast on his arm, his rabbi, Hillel Silverman, asked what had happened. Jacob replied, "In my club, somebody was very raucous, and I was the bouncer."

### *1960*

Joe Peterson had agreed to perform in one of Jacob's clubs. He was promised a handsome commission. He never received it. When the entertainer asked Jacob for his pay, Jacob punched him in the face, knocking out a front tooth.

### *September 1962*

Frank Carrero worked as a handyman at Jacob's club. One evening, he became heated and began to argue with another man. When Jacob intervened, Frank told him to back off and mind his own business. Jacob paused just long enough to allow Frank to walk to a neighboring club. When Frank turned around, Jacob was on him, beating him furiously. Soon after, Frank was in the hospital being treated for a severely damaged eye.

Jacob was always ready for a fight, and he won nearly all of them. He kept himself in fighting shape by working out at the YMCA and lifting weights at his club and apartment. Fifteen times since he moved to Dallas, he had beaten up a customer at his club with his fists or a blackjack, sometimes pistol-whipping the offending patron.

If he ever needed it, he had a pistol on hand.[213]

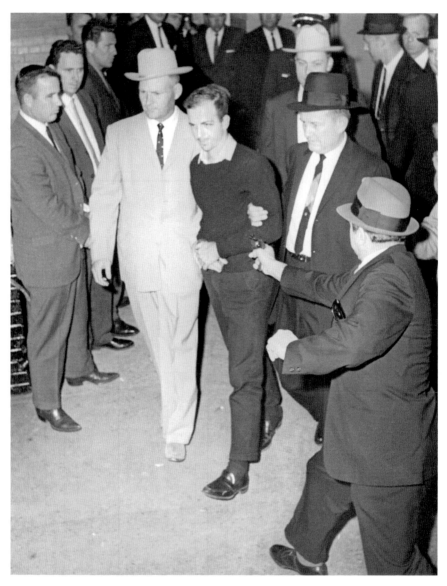

Jack Ruby a moment before shooting Lee Harvey Oswald. The photo was captured by Ira Jefferson "Jack" Beers Jr. for the *Dallas Morning News* and was subsequently published as part of the Warren Commission report. *From the* Dallas Morning News/*Wikimedia Commons.*

*November 22, 1963*
*9:50 p.m.*
*Dallas, Texas*

Jacob drove to Congregation Shearith Israel synagogue for the service for the dead. The service had begun at 8:00 p.m., but although Jacob was a proud Jew, ready to defend his faith with his fists, he was not a particularly devout Jew. (Journalist Seth Kantor summed up Jacob's religiosity: "On a scale of from 1 to 10, with 10 being a profoundly rational, philosophical approach to Judaism, [he] was a 1."[214]) He arrived at the synagogue a little before 10:00 p.m., just before the service ended. It didn't really matter. He had "a foggy mind" and couldn't "take it in fully" anyway.

There was no way Jacob was going to simply drive home and go to sleep. He was too jumpy, too shocked, too angry to do any such thing. And then an idea came to him: "In my mind suddenly it mulled over me that the police department was working overtime. I have always been very close to the police department, I don't know why." He drove to Phil's Delicatessen and ordered a dozen corned beef sandwiches and proceeded to the police station. The scene was exactly what he hoped for—chaotic and lively. "It took away the tragic feeling. I was in a complete change of mental reaction, already I am with the deal."

Despite knowing so many officers on a first-name basis, Jacob could not get in the station. Nor did they want his sandwiches. So, he told one of the guards that he was going to give the food to one of the news crews who were covering the murder from inside the station. An officer offered to locate one of the reporters. As the officer was doing so, an announcement was made that the prisoner would be taken to the basement for viewing. Jacob joined the throng of credentialed reporters flocking to the basement.

Everyone was anxiously awaiting the moment that Dallas's most recent murderer was placed before them. The five-foot-nine, 175-pound Jacob climbed a table in the back of the room. "I am standing on a table above everybody. History is being made. I even passed out some of my cards. Newsmen from all over the world were there, asking me who was this one and that one."

Finally, the prisoner was brought before the throng. Jacob was not impressed. In fact, the sight of the skinny, pasty murderer filled him with loathing and hate. "He had a very smirky expression, he looked cunning and vicious—like an animal—like a Communist. I felt like I was looking at a rat." Jacob had a loaded pistol in his pocket. He thought about using it.[215]

A police photo of Lee Harvey Oswald taken shortly after his arrest. *National Archives.*

*Early 1963*
*Dallas, Texas*

Jacob walked down the street outside his Oak Cliff apartment—the same section of town in which Herbert Noble lived and where his wife had been blown up—in the midafternoon. He felt good. He had just taken his second bath of the day and had covered his body in oils and creams. He wore a gray fedora hat to cover his thinning hair. When he thought of his hair, his blood pressure rose. He was paying trichologist Bruce McLean a decent amount of money to preserve his increasingly thinning hair. Otherwise, he was pleased with his appearance. All his work at the YMCA and the extra lifting at his club and in his apartment, not to mention his extremely healthy diet, had kept the fifty-two-year-old in relatively good shape.

Jacob got to his meticulously clean Oldsmobile. It was a slick-looking car for a slick-looking man. Everyone who saw Jacob Rubenstein knew that he was a clean, sharp man—a man of consequence. To all outward appearances, Jacob Rubenstein was a man to be envied, a man who had his life together.

Later that evening, Elnora Pitts, Jacob's maid, let herself into his house and began to straighten and clean it. She must have felt like Hercules at the Augean Stables. There were newspapers and dirty clothes all over the floor. The dishes hadn't been washed since the last time she washed them. The baseboards had been scuffed up, and couch filling was scattered over the floor and couch.

While Elnora cleaned, Jacob was meeting with Dr. Coleman Jacobson to receive treatment for his gonorrhea. Outside the office, his dog, Sheba, waited in the Oldsmobile, gnawing on the upholstery, which was all over the floorboard next to a set of brass knuckles. There was a bag of cash, handkerchiefs, a can of paint, one golf shoe, copies of newspapers, jars of food, a change of clothes, bathing cap, photos of strippers, a can of paint and scraps of paper spread throughout the car, front and back.[216]

Yes, to outward appearances, Jacob Rubenstein had it together; he was clean, disciplined and sharp. Inwardly, his life was chaos. And it was about to get a whole lot more turbulent.

*Saturday, November 23, 1963*
*4:30 a.m.*
*No. 207, 222 South Ewing, Dallas, Texas*

Jacob burst into his apartment and began to shake his sleeping roommate, George Senator. When he finally got his drunk friend awake, he began to relay the events of the past sixteen hours. "Gee, his poor children and [wife], what a terrible thing to happen.…This is the work of the John Birch Society or the Communist Party or maybe a combination of both." Jacob insisted that his roommate go for a predawn ride with him. They ended up at a coffeehouse in the Southland Hotel. Jacob was still fuming about the lowlife murderer with the look of a rat.

He also began a rant directed at an editorial he had read in yesterday morning's paper. A man named "Bernard Weissman" had made some pretty unpatriotic remarks that greatly angered Jacob Rubenstein. He had spent considerable effort trying to track down the mysterious Weissman but was thus far unsuccessful. He began to connect the dots. "Bernard Weissman" was a communist and anti-American. Even worse, he was an anti-Semite. He had signed a highly inflammatory and anti-American letter with a Jewish name to make the paper's readers distrust Jews. It was all one big conspiracy to embarrass his people, the chosen ones.

Jacob and George finally returned to their apartment early Saturday morning. George sat around in his underwear watching television while

Jacob slept the morning away. George then went downstairs to do some laundry. When he returned, Jacob was gone.[217]

JACOB LOVED HIS DOGS. He slept with women, but he treated his dogs like ladies. They went everywhere with him—to work, to restaurants, to his friends' houses. One day, he took his brood to his rabbi Hillel Silverman's house. While the two men stood outside on the porch, watching the dogs run around, Jacob turned to Silverman and began to cry: "I'm unmarried, I have no children, this is my wife [he pointed to his dachshund, Sheba] and these are my children." The rabbi thought Jacob's statement strange, but shortly after, Jacob ceased sobbing and changed the conversation as if nothing had happened.

Jacob took his car to William Serur to have the back seats upholstered. He pulled the Oldsmobile into the lot. Serur came out, greeted his customer and opened the back seat. He burst out laughing when he saw the carnage in the back seat. There was upholstery everywhere, all over the floorboard, and just shreds of the seat covers remained, springs protruding.

"What are you laughing about?"

"I want to know what did this. I've never seen seat covers like this.…What did this?"

"My children. Anything wrong with that?"

"I can't figure this out. You mean the dogs?"

"My children did it. What do you want to do, cause an argument out here? I asked you to come down here and give me a price on those seat covers, and now you want to criticize my children. I don't want you to refer to them as dogs. Those are my children. Don't you have children? Don't you respect them? I respect my kids. They go wherever I go and I want you not to call them dogs anymore."

Knowing Jacob's penchant for fighting, Serur wisely let the matter go and gave his quick-tempered customer the quote he requested.

Not long after, Serur came to Jacob's apartment to examine some furniture. When he walked in, he saw that the baseboard and couch that had been chewed up. This time, Serur didn't laugh. He only asked, "What in the world happened?" He should have anticipated the reply: "My children. Anything wrong with that? My children eat it up."[218]

*Sunday, November 24, 1963*
*11:16–11:21 a.m.*
*Dallas, Texas*

Jacob walked into the Western Union office on 2034 Main Street. He needed to wire some money to an employee. When the person in front of him finished their business, he stepped up to the teller and sent the agreed-on $25 ($26.87 after fees and tax). Jacob took his receipt and left the office, taking a left toward the police station.[219]

Less than two minutes later, he was among a crowd of onlookers in the station's basement. Four minutes after Jacob left the Western Union offices, the murderer who had incensed him nearly forty-eight hours before was led into the basement and toward a waiting automobile, where he would be transported to a more secure jail.

Jacob was surrounded by detectives, police officers and reporters, including a number of television employees who had their television lights behind Jacob and aimed at where the murderer would appear.

And appear he did, handcuffed to Detective James Robert Leavelle. Seeing his chance to "cleanse Dallas of its stain," Jacob lunged from behind one of his officer friends and toward the culprit. In an instant, he had drawn his pistol and fired point-blank into the prisoner's stomach.

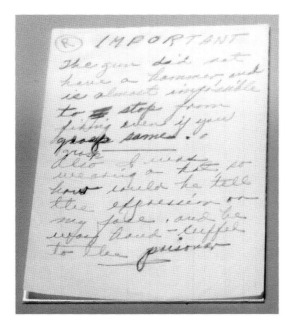

A note Jack Ruby handed to his attorney during his murder trial. *Library of Congress.*

Both men, prisoner and avenger, fell to the ground, the former with a fatal bullet in his stomach, the latter tackled by six detectives. Surprised by the immediate and forceful reaction of the detectives, "It flashed through my mind, 'Why are all these guys jumping on top of me? I'm a very known person with the police and everybody else. I'm not somebody who is a screwball.'" He cried out, "You all know me! I'm Jack Ruby!"[220]

THUS FELL LEE HARVEY Oswald, assassin of President John F. Kennedy. An hour and forty-six minutes later, Oswald would be pronounced dead at Parkland Hospital. He died in Trauma Room Two, just across the hall from the room in which his president died.[221]

Jack Ruby, who changed his name from Jacob Rubenstein when he first came to Dallas, was promptly arrested and charged with murder. On March 14, 1964, a jury convicted him, and he was sentenced to death.

During his imprisonment and trial, he insisted that he had killed Oswald for a number of reasons: he wanted to spare Mrs. Kennedy the trauma of a trial; he did it out of patriotism; he did it to restore the honor of American Jews, "to show that Jews had guts." He told Rabbi Silverman, "I did it for the Jewish people."[222]

Jacob became convinced that Jews were being persecuted across the United States because of his actions. One day, his brother and nephew came to visit. Police sirens began to go off outside, and Jacob began to shout, "You hear that? You hear that? They're torturing Jews in the basement!"

Later, Rabbi Silverman came to visit Jacob. He described the meeting: "In prison, he deteriorated psychologically. One time I walked in and he said, 'Come on, rabbi, duck underneath the table. They're pouring oil on the Jews and setting it on fire.' He was quite psychotic."[223]

A psychologist who examined Ruby between his arrest and trial, Dr. Manfred S. Guttmacher, provided the following diagnosis:

*Because of his deep-seated feelings of inadequacy he is acutely aware of his position as a member of a minority group, against which bigotry and prejudice is frequently directed. Doubtless, this was an important factor in the high regard which he had for President Roosevelt and President Kennedy. The fact that President Kennedy was, himself, a member of a minority group…had a special impact on this patient.[224]*

124

Jacob Rubenstein had avenged the murder of John F. Kennedy and, by extension, five decades worth of anti-Semitic remarks and threats. And now he paid the price for his bold action, under constant surveillance in a small prison cell. In his mind, he was a martyr for his faith. To the American public, he was a member of an underworld conspiracy that resulted in the death of a beloved president.

THE WEEKEND OF NOVEMBER 22–24, 1963, was a microcosm of Jack Ruby's life. Those three days were a replication of every day of his life. There were ups and downs, activity and depression, bantering and fighting. His caring, pugilistic, impulsive nature was on full display. So was his deteriorating mind. (Ruby was diagnosed with brain cancer when he entered Parkland Hospital with pneumonia in 1966, three years after killing Oswald. How long had the cancer been in his brain? How did that affect his prison delusions?)

While in prison, Jack Ruby survived three suicide attempts (running twenty feet and slamming his head into a wall; trying to hang himself with a pants leg; and pouring water on the ground, unscrewing a light bulb and trying to ram his finger into the light socket) and died on January 3, 1967, in Parkland Hospital due to complications from lung cancer.

His delusions continued until the very end.[225]

# EPILOGUE

T hank you for reading *Dallas Tough*. We would like to take this time to express to our readers our profound respect for Dallas and its rich history. Although this work told stories of the seamier side of the city, we do appreciate all the positive contributions Dallas has made to Texas and the United States. As we stated in the beginning, one of the intentions of this book was to encourage further scholarly development on the rich history of the city. While our goal was to bring to life the frontier mentality and the rough-and-tumble nature of the city—a city that required grit, audacity and defiance—we do hope that some future historians and storytellers will balance our stories of poverty, racism and murder with the good, the beautiful and the uplifting. Perhaps they could write the history of the Winspear Opera House, Perot Museum, Southern Methodist University or the University of Dallas, along with scores of other institutions and actors who have made Dallas one of America's cultural treasures.

# NOTES

## Part I

1. Details about Creek dress come from Paterek, *Encyclopedia of American Indian Costume*, 18–20.
2. Bidlack and Johnson, "Matthew Sparks (Died 1793)."
3. Sparks, "Descendants of William Sparks"; Brandon, "General David Blackshear"; Downes, "Creek-American Relations," 361–62; Huff, "Jonas Fauche's Role on Georgia's Frontiers," 15.
4. Young, "Indian Removal and Land Allotment," 31.
5. Sparks, "Descendants of William Sparks"; Brandon, "General David Blackshear."
6. Sparks, "Descendants of William Sparks."
7. Ibid.
8. Young, "Indian Removal and Land Allotment," 37–40.
9. Sparks, "Descendants of William Sparks"; Sparks, "Family of Col. Richard Sparks"; geographic regions described in Chapman et al., *Ecoregions of Mississippi*, and Griffith et al., *Ecoregions of Georgia*.
10. Barker, "Land Speculation as a Cause of the Texas Revolution," 76–77.
11. Ibid.; Winfrey, *Texas Indian Papers*, 19–20.
12. Daniell, "Thing that Steals the Land," 461–66.
13. Comstock, "Post Oak Savannah and Blackland Prairie Wildlife Management."
14. Those characteristics of dress were typical of the Northeast American Indian tribes, which included the Kickapoos. Paterek, *Encyclopedia of American Indian Costume*, 41–45.
15. Moore, "Telegraph."
16. Ibid.
17. Winfrey, *Texas Indian Papers*, 22–28.
18. Paterek, *Encyclopedia of American Indian Costume*, 41–45.
19. Gibson, *Kickapoos*, 3–5.

20. Ibid., 43–47.
21. Ibid., 48–51.
22. Paterek, *Encyclopedia of American Indian Costume*, 41–45.
23. Gibson, *Kickapoos*, 97–100.
24. Ibid., 143–44.
25. DeShields, *Border Wars of Texas*, 154–59, 199.
26. Daniell, "Thing that Steals the Land," 461–66.
27. Love, *History of Navarro County*, 29–35.
28. DeShields, *Border Wars of Texas*, 225–31.
29. Starling, *Land Is the Cry!*, ix–xi, 60–63, 107.
30. Ibid., 99–100.
31. Ibid., 100–103.
32. Hazel, *Dallas*, 3–4.

# Part II

33. *Austin Weekly Statesman*, "Governor Davis in Dallas," September 7, 1871.
34. Richardson, *Texas*, 280.
35. Ibid.; Brown, *History of Dallas County, Texas*, 55–56.
36. *Galveston Daily News*, "Letters from Dallas."
37. Moynehon, *Republicanism in Reconstruction Texas*, 135–36; Johnson, "State Police."
38. Enstam, "Opportunity versus Propriety," 107.
39. Denton, "Filibusterism and Catholicity," 10–11; Sam Acheson, "Mayor Henry S. Ervay Leads City," in Acheson, *Dallas Yesterday*, 152–55; Enstam, *When Dallas Became a City*.
40. *Austin Weekly Statesman*, "Governor Davis in Dallas"; *Galveston Daily News*, "Letters from Dallas."
41. *Galveston Daily News*, "Letters from Dallas."
42. Ibid.
43. Campbell, *Grass-Roots Reconstruction in Texas*, 89–90.
44. Acheson, *Dallas Yesterday*, 152–55.
45. Enstam, *When Dallas Became a City*, 58–63.
46. Acheson, *Dallas Yesterday*, 152–55.
47. Ibid.
48. Enstam, *When Dallas Became a City*, 8–10.
49. *Austin Weekly Statesman*, "Governor Davis in Dallas."
50. Enstam, *When Dallas Became a City*, 4–5.
51. Graff, *Dallas Myth*, 278–79; Enstam, "Opportunity versus Propriety," 107.
52. Enstam, "Opportunity versus Propriety," 106–7.
53. Ibid.
54. Ibid.
55. *Dallas Daily Herald*, "Iron Bridge at Dallas."
56. Cristol, "Light in the Prairie."
57. "Timeline: Dallas and Forth Worth," in *Legacies*.

58. Acheson, *Dallas Yesterday*, 152–55.

59. Ibid., 114.

60. This account is a fictionalized vision of the consumptive Doc Holliday (or any dentist with tuberculosis) performing a routine dental procedure. The prices and procedures can be found in the *Dallas Daily Herald*, April 11, 1877, and May 16, 1884.

61. Blakemore, "Disease that Helped Put Colorado on the Map"; Roberts, *Doc Holliday*, 28, 59–61.

62. Doc Holliday had a close relationship with his cousin, Martha Anne "Mattie" Holliday. The nature of their relationship is still unknown, but Mattie was one of the very few people Doc spoke openly with and stayed in touch with. Mattie eventually became a nun and was the inspiration for Margaret Mitchell's character Melanie Hamilton in *Gone with the Wind*. Roberts, *Doc Holliday*, 63.

63. It is possible that Holliday was involved in the murder of a few young Black persons who refused to leave a swimming hole that whites had claimed for themselves. Roberts, *Doc Holliday*, 66–67.

64. Roberts, *Doc Holliday*, 67. There is some dispute as to the path Holliday took to reach Dallas. From Pensacola to Galveston to Dallas seems the most likely.

65. Masterson, "Famous Gunfighters of the Western Frontier," 5–6, quoted in Roberts, *Doc Holliday*, 95.

66. *Dallas Daily Herald*, August 7, 1874.

67. *Dallas Daily Herald*, October 30, 1875.

68. *Dallas Daily Herald*, "Mayor's Court," July 20, 1875.

69. *Dallas Daily Herald*, July 9, 1875.

70. *Dallas Daily Herald*, "Mayor's Court," December 1, 1875.

71. Roberts, *Doc Holliday*, 78.

72. *Dallas Weekly Herald*, "Dallas County."

73. For an excellent description of Dallas at the time of Holliday's arrival in 1873, see Roberts, *Doc Holliday*, 68–69.

74. *Dallas Daily Herald*, "Criminal Statistics."

75. *Dallas Weekly Herald*, "Our Gambling Hells."

76. Roberts, *Doc Holliday*, 70.

77. *Dallas Daily Herald*, June 28, 1873.

78. *Dallas Daily Herald*, "Local Brevities," December 31, 1874.

79. *Dallas Daily Herald*, "An Hour with Old Tige."

80. *Dallas Daily Herald*, "Mayor's Court," December 10, 1875.

81. *Dallas Daily Herald*, "Mayor's Court," December 7, 1875.

82. *Dallas Daily Herald*, "Caught on the Fly."

83. *Dallas Daily Herald*, May 2, 1875. The same article reported that sports would know the exact hour when the keno game was to commence because a local band would begin to play a particular song.

84. *Dallas Daily Herald*, "Local Brevities," December 9, 1875.

85. Seegar's office was four blocks from Dealey Plaza, where President John F. Kennedy would be assassinated eighty-nine years later.

86. *Dallas Daily Herald*, March 27, 1874.

87. *Dallas Weekly Herald,* October 11, 1873.

88. *Dallas Weekly Herald,* January 2, 1875.

89. Roberts, *Doc Holliday,* 80–81.

90. *Dallas Weekly Herald,* July 7, 1877.

91. Roberts, *Doc Holliday,* 82.

92. It is worth noting that while in Scyene, Belle became acquainted with Cole Younger, who had made his headquarters there. Younger wrote, "In 1871, while I was herding cattle in Texas, Jim Reed and his wife, with their two children, came back to her people. Reed had run afoul of the Federal authorities for passing counterfeit money at Los Angeles and had skipped between two days. Belle told her people she was tired of roaming the country over and wanted to settle down at Syene [*sic*]. Mrs. Shirley wanted to give them part of the farm, and knowing my influence with the father, asked me to intercede in behalf of the young folks. I did, and he set them up on a farm, and I cut a lot of the calves from one of my two herds and left with them." Shirley, *Belle Starr and Her Times,* 94.

93. Ibid., 76.

94. *Dallas Daily Commercial,* February 20 and June 9, 1874.

95. Shirley, *Belle Starr and Her Times,* 107.

96. *Dallas Commercial,* July 25, 1874.

97. Shirley, *Belle Starr and Her Times,* 106.

98. House of Representatives records, Watt Grayson claim file, Exhibit G, quoted in Shirley, *Belle Starr and Her Times,* 127–28.

99. House of Representatives records, Watt Grayson claim file, Exhibit H, quoted in Shirley, *Belle Starr and Her Times,* 128.

100. Morris statement at the coroner's inquest in Paris, *Dallas Commercial,* August 10, 1874, quoted in Shirley, *Belle Starr and Her Times,* 119.

101. Biography.com, "Belle Starr."

## *Part III*

102. *Dallas Express,* "Knights of Ku Klux Klan."

103. Morris, "Saving Society through Politics."

104. U.S. Congress House Committee on Un-American Activities, "Present-Day Ku Klux Klan Movement," 2–6.

105. Ebert, "Birth of a Nation."

106. Morris, "Saving Society through Politics," 27–28; Payne, "Dallas Morning News and the Ku Klux Klan," in *Legacies,* 18; Alexander, *Ku Klux Klan in the Southwest,* 28–29.

107. Caylor, "Ku Klux Klan Brands Negro."

108. Morris, "Saving Society through Politics."

109. *Marshall News Messenger,* "Ku Klux Klan."

110. MacLean, *Behind the Mask of Chivalry,* 23–30; Dillard, "In Downtown Dallas."

111. Dallas Art Association, "Second Annual Exhibition American and European Art."

112. Caylor, "Ku Klux Klan Brands Negro."

113. Higbie, "Between Romance and Degradation," 253–65; Lacey, "Vagrancy and Other Crimes," 1,203–4; Cash, *Mind of the South,* 312–13.

114. *Waco News-Tribune,* "Won't Prosecute Ku Klux Klan."
115. U.S. Senate, *Senator from Texas,* 682–85, 1,270.
116. *El Paso Herald,* "Dallas Citizens Move to End Activities."
117. Jackson, *Ku Klux Klan in the City,* 72–73.
118. U.S. Senate, *Senator from Texas,* 1,270–71.
119. *El Paso Herald,* "Dallas Citizens Move to End Activities."
120. Alexander, *Ku Klux Klan in the Southwest,* 79–80.
121. Cadillac, "Carbolic Acid Blues."
122. *Dallas Express,* "Hundreds of Men, Women and Children." There is some debate as to whether the Hattie Burleson who killed W.E. King is the same person as the blues singer Hattie Burleson. However, the evidence seems to indicate that it is the same woman. The authors recommend for further reading Michael Corcoran, "Hattie Burleson's Dead Lovers Blues," http://www.michaelcorcoran.net/hattie-burlesons-dead-lover-blues.
123. *Dallas Express,* "Slayress of W.E. King to Be Exonerated."
124. Govenar and Brakefield, *Deep Ellum,* 10.
125. Ibid., 10.
126. Ibid., 11.
127. Ibid., 14.
128. Guinn, *Go Down Together,* 48.
129. Parker and Cowan, *Fugitives,* location 512.
130. Ibid., locations 512–18.
131. Sleeper, *I'll Do My Own Damn Killin',* 35.
132. Ibid., 35–36.
133. Parker and Cowan, *Fugitives,* location 620.
134. Bosse, "Dallas."
135. Guinn, *Go Down Together,* 53.
136. Parker and Cowan, *Fugitives,* location 590.
137. Ibid., location 590.
138. Ibid., location 610.
139. Guinn, *Go Down Together,* 48.
140. There is some dispute as to whether Bonnie actually wrote this poem or just had it in her possession. Woodward, "Clearing Up a Bonnie Poems Mix Up."
141. Guinn, *Go Down Together,* 111.
142. Parker and Cowan, *Fugitives,* location 536.
143. Texas Hideout, "Bonnie and Roy Thornton"; Guinn, *Go Down Together,* 49.
144. Parker and Cowan, *Fugitives,* location 579.
145. Ibid., location 590, January 1, 1928.
146. Ibid., location 590, January 3, 1928.
147. Ibid., location 590, January 3, 1928.
148. Ibid., location 610, January 7, 1928.
149. Ibid., location 598, January 5, 1928.
150. *Abilene Reporter-News,* "Vigilant Texas Prison Guards."
151. Parker and Cowan, *Fugitives,* location 680.
152. Ibid., location, 576.

153. Govenar and Brakefield, *Deep Ellum*, 69.
154. Parker and Cowan, *Fugitives*, location 552.
155. Guinn, *Go Down Together*, 192–93.
156. Ibid., 80–81.
157. Ibid., 217.
158. Ibid., 225.
159. Ibid., 240–41.
160. Ibid., 2–5, 283.
161. Ibid., 365.
162. The most thorough narrative of the murder of Brooks Coffman was produced by Martha Martin of the *New York Daily News* several days after the fact. Martin's narrative is comprehensive and dramatic and seems to be mostly accurate, although some minor details conflict with other reporters' accounts from the time. Martin, *New York Daily News*, "Blonde Sweetheart Ends 6-Year Affair." A fuller picture of Brooks Coffman's life can be obtained from city directories, census records, a draft card and Brooks's death certificate: Dallas, Texas City Directory, 1930; U.S. Selective Service System, World War I Selective Service System Draft Registration Cards, 1917–18, Registration State: Texas, Registration County: Collin, Roll: 1952339, Draft Board: 2; Texas Department of State Health Services, "Brooks Coffman"; U.S. Bureau of the Census, Fifteenth Census of the United States, 1930, Census Place: Dallas, Texas, Page: 10A, Enumeration District: 0082, FHL microfilm: 2342053.
163. U.S. Bureau of the Census, Fifteenth Census of the United States, 1930, T626, 2,667 rolls, Year: 1930, Census Place: Dallas, Texas, Page: 36B, Enumeration District: 0093, FHL microfilm: 2342054; "U.S., School Yearbooks, 1880–2012," School Name: Sunset High School, Year: 1931; Martin, "Blonde Sweetheart Ends 6-Year Affair."
164. Martin, "Blonde Sweetheart Ends 6-Year Affair."
165. McElhaney, "Dallas 1933," in *Legacies*, 26–33.
166. Biles, "Urban South in the Great Depression," 71–100; McElhaney, "Dallas 1933," in *Legacies*, 26–33.
167. McElhaney, "Dallas 1933," in *Legacies*, 26–33.
168. Martin, "Blonde Sweetheart Ends 6-Year Affair."
169. Stephenson, "Corinne Maddox at Home."
170. *Austin American-Statesman*, "Assault to Murder Is Charged Dallas Lawyer."
171. Martin, "Blonde Sweetheart Ends 6-Year Affair"; *Corpus Christi Caller-Times*, "Dallas Attorney Shot to Death."
172. Dickson, "Top-Break Backups."
173. Workman, "Dillinger Gun."
174. Texas Department of Health, Bureau of Vital Statistics, Brooks Coffman, Standard Certificate of Death.
175. Stephenson, "Corinne Maddox at Home."
176. *Shreveport Times*, "Dallas Jury Deliberates Honor Death."
177. *Herald-Journal*, "Beauty Wrote Poem of Hate."

## Part IV

178. Cartwright, "Benny and the Boys."

179. Sleeper, *I'll Do My Own Damn Killin'*, 67–68.

180. *Denton Record-Chronicle*, "Questioning Fails to Reveal Denton Man's Assailant."

181. Sleeper, *I'll Do My Own Damn Killin'*, 84.

182. Ibid., 65.

183. Ibid., 105–6.

184. *Denton Record-Chronicle*, "Herbert Noble Again Survives"; Sleeper, *I'll Do My Own Damn Killin'*, 118.

185. The "contract" on Noble's life is, to this day, vague. There is no doubt that Benny Binion was behind a number of these assassination attempts. Other attempts were very likely instigated by some of Noble's other enemies in Dallas. Still others may have been opportunistic, would-be assassins hoping to collect a payday. Word was definitely out that Binion would be more than pleased to read of the death of his adversary—and he had the money to express his gratitude. He began by offering a $10,000 bounty, then $25,000 and then $50,000. Cartwright, "Benny and the Boys."

186. *The Monitor*, "Bomb Blast Death Probed"; Sleeper, *I'll Do My Own Damn Killin'*, 125–26.

187. *Galveston Daily News*, "Funeral Is Held For Mrs. Noble."

188. *Pampa Daily News*, "Green Lived in World of Own."

189. *Odessa American*, "Ex-Con Cut Down by Hail of Lead"; Sleeper, *I'll Do My Own Damn Killin'*, 133–37.

190. *Pampa Daily News*, "Gambler Is Injured for Sixth Time."

191. *Denton Record-Chronicle*, "Herbert Noble Is Ambushed"; Sleeper, *I'll Do My Own Damn Killin'*, 143–45.

192. *The Monitor*, "Dallas Gambler Escapes Bullet"; Sleeper, *I'll Do My Own Damn Killin'* 145–46.

193. Sleeper, *I'll Do My Own Damn Killin'*, 159–62.

194. *Denton Record-Chronicle*, "Sheriff Indicates New Leads"; Sleeper, *I'll Do My Own Damn Killin'*, 162–63. The two assailants, in this particular case, were likely not hired by Benny Binion. However, word of a now $50,000 reward had spread throughout the Dallas underworld. One of the foremost historians of the Dallas Gambling War, Gary W. Sleeper, claimed, "By the early fall of 1950, planning to kill Herbert Noble had practically become a cottage industry in Dallas and Fort Worth." Sleeper, *I'll Do My Own Damn Killin'*, 164.

195. Sleeper, *I'll Do My Own Damn Killin'*, 170.

196. *Austin American-Statesman*, "Dallas' Well-Shot-at Noble Arrested"; Sleeper, *I'll Do My Own Damn Killin'*, 177–88.

197. *Corpus Christi Caller-Times*, "Blast Rocks Private Club"; Sleeper, *I'll Do My Own Damn Killin'*, 180–81.

198. *Waxahachie Daily Light*, "Herbert Noble Escaped Tenth Attempt on Life."

199. *Corpus Christi Caller-Times*, "Plane Blast Fails to Kill Herbert Noble"; Sleeper, *I'll Do My Own Damn Killin'*, 183.

200. *Longview News-Journal*, "Noble Survives 11th Attempt"; Sleeper, *I'll Do My Own Damn Killin'*, 184.

201. *Denton Record-Chronicle*, "Noble Killed in 12th Try on Life"; Sleeper, *I'll Do My Own Damn Killin'*, 193–95.

202. Cartwright, "Benny and the Boys."

203. *D Magazine*, "Dallas Crime through the Decades."

204. Ruby's description, given by him to the Warren Commission, June 7, 1964, quoted in Kantor, *Who Was Jack Ruby?*, 40.

205. Kantor, *Who Was Jack Ruby?*, 38–40.

206. Warren Commission Report, 781–84.

207. "Preliminary Diagnostic Impression of Jack Ruby," 2.

208. Kantor, *Who Was Jack Ruby?*, 41–42.

209. Ibid., 99.

210. Ibid., 106–7.

211. Ibid., 42–43.

212. "Preliminary Diagnostic Impression of Jack Ruby," 3; Kantor, *Who Was Jack Ruby?*, 43.

213. Each of the aforementioned incidents is documented in either the Warren Commission Report, 796–97, 804–5, or in North, "Remembering JFK." Always quick to fights, especially when his Jewish roots were mocked—as illustrated by the incidents surrounding his early adulthood—these incidents show his hot-tempered and volatile nature. The world would soon be made aware of both.

214. Kantor, *Who Was Jack Ruby?*, 5.

215. "Preliminary Diagnostic Impression of Jack Ruby," 4; Kantor, *Who Was Jack Ruby?*, 46–48.

216. Kantor, *Who Was Jack Ruby?*, 29, 171, 174.

217. Ibid., 51–52.

218. Ibid., 172–74.

219. Testimony of Doyle E. Lane.

220. Kantor, *Who Was Jack Ruby?*, 68–73.

221. O'Reilly and Duggard, *Killing Kennedy*, 290.

222. North, "My History with the Family of Lee Harvey Oswald's Killer."

223. Ibid.

224. "Preliminary Diagnostic Impression of Jack Ruby," 2.

225. The authors would be remiss not to mention the myriad conspiracy theories surrounding the Ruby-Oswald-JFK saga. We believe we've accurately portrayed the character of Jacob Rubenstein, or Jack Ruby: militantly proud of his Jewish roots but also hot-tempered and violent. We also acknowledge his connections—pertinent or not—to the mafia and Dallas police force, as well as to other forces capable of such a high-profile assassination. Was Jack Ruby working for one of these organizations? Possibly. With all due respect to other, far more qualified researchers, is there conclusive evidence? No. Could any of these organizations have used a person like Jack Ruby? You betcha. But did they?

# BIBLIOGRAPHY

## *Albums*

Cadillac, Bobby. *Carbolic Acid Blues.* Columbia Records, December 8, 1928. Genius. https://genius.com/Bobby-cadillac-carbolic-acid-blues-lyrics.

## *Maps*

Chapman, Shannen S., et al. *Ecoregions of Mississippi.* 1:1,000,000. Reston, VA: U.S. Geological Survey, 2004.

Griffith, Glenn E., et al. *Ecoregions of Georgia.* 1:1,500,000. Corvallis, OR: U.S. Environmental Protection Agency, 2001.

## *Articles*

*Abilene Reporter-News.* "Vigilant Texas Prison Guards Foil Attempted Break by 27 Felons: Two Slain, Two Are Wounded in Eastham Battle." October 4, 1937.

*Austin American-Statesman.* "Assault to Murder Is Charged Dallas Lawyer." May 22, 1939.

———. "Dallas' Well-Shot-at Noble Arrested After Fight with Man Over a Carbine." January 24, 1951

*Austin Weekly Statesman.* "Governor Davis in Dallas." September 7, 1871.

Barker, Eugene C. "Land Speculation as a Cause of the Texas Revolution." *Texas Historical Association Quarterly* 10, no. 1 (n.d.): 76–77.

Bidlack, Russell, and William P. Johnson. "Matthew Sparks (Died 1793) of North Carolina and Georgia: A Biographical Sketch." *Sparks Quarterly* 9, no. 2 (1961).

Biles, Roger. "The Urban South in the Great Depression." *Journal of Southern History* 56, no. 1 (1990).

Biography.com. "Belle Starr." https://www.biography.com/personality/belle-starr.

Blakemore, Erin. "The Disease that Helped Put Colorado on the Map." History Stories. https://www.history.com.

Bosse, Paula. "Dallas: 'Amusement Capital of the Southwest—1946.'" Flashback: Dallas. https://flashbackdallas.com/2016/01/19/amusement-capital-of-the-southwest-1946.

Brandon, Linda B. "General David Blackshear and the Georgia Frontier during the Early 1800s." *Proceedings and Papers of the Georgia Association of Historians* 11 (1990).

Cartwright, Gary. "Benny and the Boys: Sure They Were Gangsters but They Were Our Gangsters." *Texas Monthly*, October 1991. https://www.texasmonthly.com/articles/benny-and-the-boys.

Caylor, Harry. "Ku Klux Klan Brands Negro." *Oklahoma News*, April 2, 1921.

Comstock, Jeffrey A. "Post Oak Savannah and Blackland Prairie Wildlife Management: Historical Perspective." Descriptions of the Level IV Ecoregions of Texas, 2004. Texas Parks and Wildlife Department, U.S. Geological Survey. https://tpwd.texas.gov/landwater/land/habitats/post_oak.

*Corpus Christi Caller-Times*. "Blast Rocks Private Club of Dallas Gambler." February 13, 1951.

———. "Dallas Attorney Shot to Death on Street by Woman." November 20, 1939.

———. "Plane Blast Fails to Kill Herbert Noble." March 24, 1951.

Cristol, Gerry. "A Light in the Prairie: On the Trail of the Iron Horse." *Western States Jewish History* 31 (1998).

Dallas Art Association. "Second Annual Exhibition American and European Art." 1921.

*Dallas Daily Herald*. "Caught on the Fly," August 28, 1875.

———. "Criminal Statistics," October 30, 1875.

———. "An Hour with Old Tige," November 12, 1875.

———. "The Iron Bridge at Dallas." December 30, 1871.

*Dallas Express*. "Hundreds of Men, Women and Children, Black and White View Body of Editor W.E. King, Who Was Shot to Death with a Revolver at the Hands of Hattie Burleson. Slayress Held without Bail. State and Nation Mourn the Loss." August 30, 1919.

———. "Knights of Ku Klux Klan Parade the Streets of Dallas." May 28, 1921.

———. "Slayress of W.E. King to Be Exonerated." October 4, 1919.

*Dallas Weekly Herald*. "Dallas County: Its Social and Political Condition." March 15, 1873.

———. "Our Gambling Hells." November 21, 1874.

Daniell, Forrest. "The Thing that Steals the Land." *Surveying and Mapping* (January–March 1955).

Denton, Andrew. "Filibusterism and Catholicity: Narciso Lopez, William Walker, and the Antebellum Struggle for America's Souls." *U.S. Catholic Historian* 33, issue 4 (2015).

*Denton Record-Chronicle*. "Herbert Noble Again Survives Hot Gun Battle." September 8, 1949.

————. "Herbert Noble Is Ambushed." January 1, 1950.

————. "Noble Killed in 12th Try on Life." August 8, 1951.

————. "Questioning Fails to Reveal Denton Man's Assailant." January 18, 1946.

————. "Sheriff Indicates New Leads in Attempt on Noble's Life." June 14, 1950.

Dickson, Jim. "Top-Break Backups." *Gunslingers—Firearms of the Old West* (Winter/Spring 2016).

Dillard, Coshandra. "In Downtown Dallas, a Crowd of 5,000 Watched This Black Man Get Lynched—and They Took Souvenirs." Timeline. https://timeline.com/allen-brooks-dallas-lynching-4fc9132ee422.

*D Magazine.* "Dallas Crime through the Decades: What the Numbers Say About Crimes in Our City Since 1945" (January 2016).

Downes, Randolph C. "Creek-American Relations, 1790–1795." *Journal of Southern History* 8, no. 3 (1942).

Ebert, Roger. "The Birth of a Nation." https://www.rogerebert.com/reviews/great-movie-the-birth-of-a-nation-1915.

*El Paso Herald.* "Dallas Citizens Move to End Activities of Lawless Bands Who Threaten, Torture 65 Men." March 29, 1922.

Enstam, Elizabeth York. "Opportunity versus Propriety: The Life and Career of Frontier Matriarch Sarah Horton Cockrell." *Frontiers: A Journal of Women Studies* 6, no. 3 (1981).

*Galveston Daily News.* "Funeral Is Held for Mrs. Noble." December 2, 1949.

————. "Letters from Dallas." May 12, 1872.

*Herald-Journal.* "Beauty Wrote Poem of Hate to Lawyer She Murdered." November 21, 1939.

Higbie, Frank Tobias. "Between Romance and Degradation: Navigating the Meanings of Vagrancy in North America, 1870–1940." In *Cast Out: Vagrancy and Homelessness in Global and Historical Perspective.* Athens: Ohio University Press, 2008.

Huff, Lawrence. "Jonas Fauche's Role on Georgia's Frontiers, 1786–1796." *Atlanta History* 34, no. 3 (1990).

Johnson, John G. "State Police." Texas State Historical Association. https://tshaonline.org/handbook/online/articles/jls02.

Lacey, Forrest W. "Vagrancy and Other Crimes of Personal Condition." *Harvard Law Review* 66, issue 7 (1953).

*Legacies: A History Journal for Dallas and North Central Texas* 11, no. 1. "Timeline: Dallas and Forth Worth." (1999).

*Longview News-Journal.* "Noble Survives 11th Attempt: Jellied Nitro Found in Engine Cylniders [*sic*]." March 28, 1951.

*Marshall News Messenger.* "The Ku Klux Klan." May 25, 1921.

Martin, Martha. "Blonde Sweetheart Ends 6-Year Affair with 2-Gun Attack." *New York Daily News*, November 26, 1939.

Masterson, William Barclay. "Famous Gunfighters of the Western Frontier: Doc Holliday." *Human Life* (May 1907).

McElhaney, Jachie. "Dallas 1933: Rock Bottom of the Great Depression." *Legacies: A History Journal for Dallas and North Central Texas* 25, no. 2 (2013).

*The Monitor.* "Bomb Blast Death Probed." November 30, 1949.

———. "Dallas Gambler Escapes Bullet in Seventh Attempt on His Life." February 7, 1950.

Moore, Francis, Jr., ed. "Telegraph." *Telegraph and Texas Register*, May 2, 1838.

North, Steve. "My History with the Family of Lee Harvey Oswald's Killer." Texas Jewish Post. http://tjpnews.com/remembering-jfk.

———. "Remembering JFK." Texas Jewish Post, November 21, 2013. http://tjpnews.com/remembering-jfk.

*Odessa American.* "Ex-Con Cut Down by Hail of Lead After Yule Party." December 25, 1949.

*Pampa Daily News.* "Gambler Is Injured for Sixth Time." January 2, 1950.

———. "Green Lived in World of Own." December 28, 1949.

Payne, Darwin. "The Dallas Morning News and the Ku Klux Klan." *Legacies: A History Journal for Dallas and North Central Texas* 9, no. 1 (1997).

"Preliminary Diagnostic Impression of Jack Ruby by Dr. Manfred S. Guttmacher, January 7, 1964." Portal to Texas History. https://texashistory.unt.edu/ark:/67531/metapth190059/m1/3.

*Shreveport Times.* "Dallas Jury Deliberates Honor Death." November 22, 1939.

Sparks, Paul E. "The Descendants of William Sparks (1761–1848)." *Sparks Quarterly* 33, no. 2 (1985).

Sparks, Sadie Greening. "The Family of Col. Richard Sparks." Genealogical research published on sadiesparks.com. 2000. http://www.sadiesparks.com/richardsparks.htm.

Stephenson, Bess. "Corinne Maddox at Home to Get 'Real Night's Sleep,'" *Fort Worth Star-Telegram*, November 21, 1939.

Testimony of Doyle E. Lane. Kennedy Assassination Home Page. http://mcadams.posc.mu.edu/russ/testimony/lane_d.htm.

Texas Hideout. "Bonnie and Roy Thornton." http://texashideout.tripod.com/bonroy.html.

U.S. Congress House Committee on Un-American Activities. "The Present-Day Ku Klux Klan Movement." Report, Ninetieth Congress, First Session, Part 1. Washington, D.C., 1967.

*Waco News-Tribune.* "Won't Prosecute Ku Klux Klan for Punishing Negro in Dallas." April 3, 1921.

Warren Commission Report. https://www.archives.gov/research/jfk/warren-commission-report/appendix-16.html#intro.

*Waxahachie Daily Light.* "Herbert Noble Escaped Tenth Attempt on Life." March 25, 1951.

Woodward, A. Winston. "Clearing Up a Bonnie Poems Mix Up—Or It's Guinn and Toland, 2 Peas in a Pod." Bonnie and Clyde History. August 29, 2009. http://bonnieandclydehistory.blogspot.com/2009/08/clearing-up-bonnie-poems-mix-up-or.html.

Workman, Dave. "The Dillinger Gun." *Gunslingers of the Gangster Era* (Fall 2015).

Young, Mary E. "Indian Removal and Land Allotment: The Civilized Tribes and Jacksonian Justice." *American Historical Review* 64, no. 1 (1958).

# Books

Acheson, Sam. *Dallas Yesterday*. Dallas, TX: SMU Press, 1977.

Alexander, Charles C. *The Ku Klux Klan in the Southwest*. Lexington: University of Kentucky Press, 1965.

Brown, John Henry. *History of Dallas County, Texas: From 1837 to 1887*. Dallas, TX: Milligan, Cornett & Farnham, 1887.

Campbell, Randolph B. *Grass-Roots Reconstruction in Texas, 1865–1880*. Baton Rouge: Louisiana State University Press, 1997.

Cash, W.J. *The Mind of the South*. New York: Knopf, 1941.

DeShields, James T. *Border Wars of Texas*. Austin, TX: State House Press, 1993.

Enstam, Elizabeth York, ed. *When Dallas Became a City: Letters of John Milton McCoy, 1870–1871*. Dallas, TX: Dallas Historical Society, 1982.

Fox, Richard. *Bella Starr the Bandit Queen: Or the Female Jesse James*. Austin, TX: Steck Company, 1960.

Gibson, Arrell Morgan. *The Kickapoos: Lords of the Middle Border*. Norman: University of Oklahoma Press, 1963.

Govenar, Alan, and Jay Brakefield. *Deep Ellum: The Other Side of Dallas*. College Station: Texas A&M Press, 2013.

Graff, Hervey. *The Dallas Myth*. Minneapolis: University of Minnesota Press, 2008.

Guinn, Jeff. *Go Down Together: The True, Untold Story of Bonnie & Clyde*. New York: Simon & Schuster, 2009.

Hazel, Michael. *Dallas: A History of "Big D."* Austin: Texas State Historical Association, 1997.

Jackson, Kenneth T. *The Ku Klux Klan in the City: 1915–1930*. New York: Oxford University Press, 1967.

Kantor, Seth. *Who Was Jack Ruby? The Startling, Until-Now Unrevealed Facts about Jack Ruby's Ties to the FBI, the CIA, and Organized Crime*. USA: Everest House, 1978.

Love, Annie Carpenter. *History of Navarro County*. Dallas, TX: Southwest Press, 1933.

MacLean, Nancy. *Behind the Mask of Chivalry: The Making of the Second Ku Klux Klan*. New York: Oxford University Press, 1994.

Moynehon, Carl H. *Republicanism in Reconstruction Texas*. Austin: University of Texas Press, 1980.

O'Reilly, Bill, and Martin Duggard. *Killing Kennedy: The End of Camelot*. New York: Henry Holt and Company, 2012.

Parker, Emma, and Nell Barrow Cowan. *Fugitives: The True Story of Clyde Barrow and Bonnie Parker*. N.p.: Wildhorse Press, 2013. Kindle edition.

Paterek, Josephine. *Encyclopedia of American Indian Costume*. New York: W.W. Norton and Company, 1994.

Richardson, Rupert Norval. *Texas: The Lone Star State*. New York: Prentice Hall, 1948.

Roberts, Gary L. *Doc Holliday: The Life and Legend*. USA: John Wiley & Sons Inc., 2006.

Shirley, Glenn. *Belle Starr and Her Times: The Literature, the Facts, and the Legends*. Norman: University of Oklahoma Press, 1982.

Sleeper, Gary W. *I'll Do My Own Damn Killin': Benny Binion, Herbert Noble, and the Texas Gambling War*. Fort Lee, NJ: Barricade Books, 2006.

Starling, Susanne. *Land Is the Cry!* Austin: Texas State Historical Association, 1998.

U.S. Senate. *Senator from Texas: Hearings Before the United States Senate Committee on Privileges and Elections, Subcommittee on S. Res. 97, Sixty-Eighth Congress, Parts 1–5.* Washington, D.C.: U.S. Government Printing Office, 1924.

Winfrey, Dorman H. *Texas Indian Papers, 1825–1843.* Austin: Texas State Library, 1959.

## Dissertations

Morris, Mark N. "Saving Society through Politics: The Ku Klux Klan Plan in Dallas, Texas, in the 1920s." PhD dissertation, University of North Texas, 1997.

## Newspapers

*Abilene Reporter-News (Abilene, Texas).*
*Austin American-Statesman (Austin, Texas).*
*Corpus Christi Caller-Times.*
*Dallas Commercial.*
*Dallas Daily Herald.*
*Dallas Express.*
*Dallas Weekly Herald.*
*Denton Record-Chronicle.*
*Galveston Daily News.*
*Longview News-Journal (Longview, Texas).*
*The Monitor (McAllen, Texas).*
*Odessa American (Odessa, Texas).*
*Pampa Daily News (Pampa, Texas).*
*Waxahachie Daily Light.*

## Miscellaneous

Dallas, Texas City Directory, 1930. U.S. City Directories, 1822–1995. Provo, UT. Accessed via Ancestry.com.

Texas Department of Health, Bureau of Vital Statistics. Brooks Coffman, Standard Certificate of Death, November 20, 1939.

Texas Department of State Health Services. "Brooks Coffman." Texas Death Certificates, 1903–82. Austin, Texas. Accessed via Ancestry.com.

U.S. Bureau of the Census. Fifteenth Census of the United States, 1930. T626, 2,667 rolls. Census place: Dallas, Texas; page: 10A; enumeration district: 0082; FHL microfilm: 2342053. Washington, D.C.: National Archives and Records Administration, 1930.

U.S. Selective Service System. Registration state: Texas; registration county: Collin; roll: 1952339; draft board: 2. World War I Selective Service System draft registration cards, 1917–18. Washington, D.C.: National Archives and Records Administration.

"U.S., School Yearbooks, 1880–2012." Sunset High School, 1931. Accessed via Ancestry.com.

# ABOUT THE AUTHORS

 JOSH FOREMAN is from Jackson, Mississippi. His second home is Seoul, South Korea, where he lived, taught, and traveled from 2005 to 2014. He holds degrees from Mississippi State University and the University of New Hampshire. He lives in Starkville, Mississippi, with his wife, Melissa, and his two children, Keeland and Genevieve. He teaches journalism at Mississippi State University.

RYAN STARRETT was birthed and reared in Jackson, Mississippi. After receiving degrees from the University of Dallas, Adams State University and Spring Hill College, as well as spending a ten-year hiatus in Texas, he has returned home to continue his teaching career. He lives in Madison with his wife, Jackie, and two children, Joseph Padraic and Penelope Rose.

*Learn more at Foremanstarrett.com.*

*Visit us at*
www.historypress.com